1001 WAYS TO HUMILIATE YOURSELF AND OTHERS

TO CAUSE EMBARRASSMENT
WHEREVER YOU GO

FIONA J. BOWRON

For Peter and Amy

First published in 2004 by
New Holland Publishers (UK) Ltd
London * Cape Town * Sydney * Auckland
www.newhollandpublishers.com

Garfield House
86–88 Edgware Road
London W2 2EA, United Kingdom

80 McKenzie Street
Cape Town 8001, South Africa

Level 1, Unit 4
Suite 411, 14 Aquatic Drive
Frenchs Forest, NSW 2086, Australia

218 Lake Road
Northcote, Auckland, New Zealand

2 4 6 8 10 9 7 5 3 1

Copyright in text © 2004 Fiona Bowron
Copyright © 2004 New Holland Publishers (UK) Ltd

All rights reserved. No part of this publication may be reproduced, stored in a retrieval system, or transmitted in any form or by any means, electronic, mechanical, or otherwise, without the prior written permission of the copyright holders and publishers.

ISBN 1 84330 855 X

Senior Editor: Clare Sayer
Design: Paul Wright
Production: Hazel Kirkman
Editorial Direction: Rosemary Wilkinson

Printed and bound by Times Offset (M) Sdn Bhd, Malaysia

DISCLAIMER

The Author and The Publishers and its Agents and Vendors accept no responsibility whatsoever for any ill health, injuries or fatalities arising from, or related to, usage of this book.

CONTENTS

Introduction 4

Chapter 1 – Work 9

Chapter 2 – Relationships 20

Chapter 3 – Children 30

Chapter 4 – Recreation And Leisure 41

Chapter 5 – House Renovations 52

Chapter 6 – Transport 61

Chapter 7 – Modern Technology 70

Chapter 8 – Other People 79

Chapter 9 – Inner Humiliation 88

And Finally… 96

INTRODUCTION

*Humiliating yourself is one of those things that
really ought to be done with style.*

According to my glossy new dictionary, to humiliate is "to lower in self-esteem". A somewhat older dictionary which also graces my cluttered bookshelf gives the definition as "to humble". They didn't have self-esteem back in those days, I suppose; and being humble probably wasn't an entirely bad thing. Nowadays, however, in the Age of the Self-Help Book, the lifestyle gurus tell us that self-esteem is everything. If you don't have self-esteem you may as well go the whole hog and not bother with all the other essentials like digital cameras, electronic organisers and cable television.

So, if self-esteem is so important, why would anyone want to read a book that tells us the opposite of what the lifestyle gurus would have us believe? An anti-lifestyle book, if you will.

And, perhaps more to the point, why would anyone need such a book? If all these self-help books are really necessary to tell us how to do it right, surely that means that we're currently doing it wrong, and we certainly don't need any help in that department, thank you very much?

If only it were that simple.

Received wisdom has it that humiliation is a bad thing (at least for the person it's happening to – let's face it, for everyone watching, it's fantastic entertainment). There is, however, a school of thought which holds that humiliation can actually be a good thing. It's not a very large school, and probably not one that you'd fight to have your children attend, but it's there. It exists.

Eastern mystics generally hold that enlightenment can only be attained without the interference of ego. Which brings us full circle back to the being humbled thing.

I'm not suggesting that you should actively seek to be humbled or even humiliated. Indeed; if you do make a deliberate attempt at self-humiliation, I suspect it wouldn't count. I am merely postulating that if (and most likely, *when*) it happens, you should remember that it's not necessarily all bad.

Seekers on the Path to True Enlightenment have long been searching for an ego-less state of being, little realising that such a state is not only within our grasp, but would in fact rush up and hit us slap bang in the face if we could only stop worrying about the next generation of mobile phones long enough to notice.

The basic problem is that we're approaching the Enlightenment issue from entirely the wrong angle. We follow the lifestyle gurus in pursuit of the impossible goal of achieving an ordered and organised life (and for our next trick we'll try turning lead into gold). We buy their books, watch their television programmes, and attend their seminars. The ironing piles up as we do so, but we cling pitifully to the belief that this time it will work. We are never aware of the futility of the whole process, and when it fails we simply move on to the next lifestyle guru. We are missing the point. Order is not a pre-requisite for a happy and satisfied life, and nor is self-esteem on the shopping list for Enlightenment.

How do you define a state of being without ego? Well, a state of humiliation comes pretty close to the mark. Humiliating yourself is one of those things that really ought to be done with style. There's no point in humiliating yourself just a little. No, if humiliating yourself is something in which you have an interest, perhaps even a talent, then you owe it to yourself to learn how to do it right. So there we have it – Total Humiliation: The only state from which True Enlightenment can be achieved.

The natural state of humankind is chaotic. Look around you. How else can you explain the income tax system?

Imposing order and rigid structure on our lives is not only unrealistic, but actually goes against nature. This is why so many of us are unhappy – we are trying to do something our species is simply not built for, and cannot hope to achieve.

The truth of this statement is demonstrated on a daily basis to anyone with a mind open enough to see it. Behaviour patterns, for example, persist only as long as it takes you to recognise the pattern and decide to take advantage of it. Hence, your children's friends, who never call round before 10am on a Saturday, will nevertheless call at 8.45am on the one morning when you have staggered half-naked into the kitchen for your first cup of tea. You will turn and slowly focus your bleary eyes on the door, with its large pane of clear glass (frosted glass is no good at all for self-humiliation – remember this), and there you will see a group of three or four small children rigid with fear at the semi-clothed creature before them, resplendent with excess fat and flab in all the right places (and body hair in all the wrong places). When control of their limbs returns they will run off giggling and screaming and proceed to tell all their friends, and you will be left unable to look your neighbours in the face for months.

Similarly, an employer who regularly monitors your work on the fifteenth of the month will inexplicably change to the day you arrive late and hung-over.

I put it to you, oh Seeker on the Path, that what we should really be doing is embracing humiliation. Let's face it; we're so much better at it than we are at turning up for meetings on time.

- *Do you panic when there's a knock at the door, and rush around frantically tidying up before you dare answer it?*
- *Does it always rain after you wash your car?*
- *Have you ever had strange looks from people on the bus, and found out later that the zip on your trousers is broken?*
- *Do you usually arrive late for things?*
- *Have you ever said something incredibly witty or intelligent and nobody noticed?*
- *Have you ever said something incredibly stupid and ridiculous and everybody noticed?*
- *Have you ever accidentally pressed the wrong button on a computer and erased three weeks' worth of work?*
- *Did your manager find out?*
- *Have you ever found yourself wondering why people are staring at you and then realised you were singing out loud?*
- *Do you ever wonder if the Inland Revenue are taking the mickey?*
- *Do you think they're all in it together?*

If you answered yes to more than three of the questions above you can breathe easy in the safe and certain knowledge that you are already a good few miles along the Path to Enlightenment. The universe clearly has it in for you, and some omnipotent being is furnishing you with endless opportunities to progress along the Great Path. Do not reject this gift. Embrace it. Soon you, too, can achieve a state of Total Humiliation.

Chapter 1
Work

One quick way to speed your journey along the path to Total Humiliation is to have your partner, or some vague acquaintance, send you a strip-o-gram on your first day.

Inspiration

- If you are not sure where you want to go, no amount of planning will get you there. Even if you do know, you'll probably lose the plan.
- The only thing preventing you achieving your goals is yourself. And a lack of money. And talent. And charisma. And skill.
- You cannot guarantee that tomorrow will come. But you can guarantee your boss will come in just as you start a personal call.
- Nothing in life is certain, so don't bet on it. Instead, bet on the 3.30 at Haydock.
- You are everything you think you are. God help the hypochondriacs.
- Whatever goes in will strongly resemble whatever comes out. This is particularly true of curry.
- Surround yourself with successful, positive and enthusiastic people (who won't want to have anything to do with the likes of you).
- If at first you don't succeed, keep going until you've made a complete idiot of yourself.

Application

- Make a habit of being late.
- Remember to schedule play time into your diary (even if your boss thinks you should be in a meeting instead).
- Check your typing thoroghly...thourogh...tho...carefully before you submit it.
- Define your goals clearly. Instead of saying, "I want to be a rock," quantify what it actually means to be a rock. (Erm... Shouldn't that be rock star? - Ed).
- Learn the art of procrastination. This will prove to be of great benefit when it comes to, say, submitting your Income Tax Returns.
- Do only one thing at a time. This does not apply to working mums, who will be expected to do at least seven things at a time.

The interview

The job interview is a perfect opportunity for Seekers on the Path to take that first tentative step towards Total Humiliation. It helps to have spent the previous night out clubbing, so you look and feel utterly dreadful for that important interview.

Remember to set off late so you are sure to arrive feeling harassed and with no time to spare. Don't worry about the parking – large companies rarely have sufficient parking spaces for their staff so you'll have to battle it out with the tea lady and finally leave your car in an unauthorised spot. At this point, if the Security Guard is any good, he'll rush out of the building waving his arms around and yelling at you. Smile sweetly and say something in Spanish. This will confuse him long enough for you to slip into the building. Your car will have been clamped and possibly towed away by the time you get back, and if this can be done in the presence of your prospective employer, so much the better.

During the interview you will be subjected to a series of questions designed to expose your strengths and weaknesses. It is considered extremely bad form to lie, although it is practically compulsory to exaggerate your talents. The depths of this exaggeration will only become an issue when you are asked for a demonstration; and this is also the point at which the probability of you being humbled is at maximum capacity.

In your search for Enlightenment, you will, of course, reply truthfully, perhaps even bluntly, when they ask how you perform under pressure. If this involves a ten-minute diatribe on the injustice of managers who sit and read the paper while their employees run around like small flying insects with startlingly blue rear-ends, do not worry.

The interviewer may well outline some sort of problem you might be expected to encounter in the job, and ask what action you would take. For example, say you were applying for a job in a theatre, "The curtain rises in ten minutes. You have a queue of customers going out of the door, through the car park and back into the local shopping centre. You have to input all of their details into the computer and get them seated before the show starts, and you have to do it alone. How would you accomplish this?" Try any or all of the following for optimum results:

"I don't know."
"I don't care."
"You tell me."

"It seems to me a problem like this is indicative poor management structure, so I'd recommend that you be sacked immediately."

In some interviews they will expect you to sit a skills test. Here, a panel of senior managers will take a twisted delight in watching you try to work out the square root of minus one using only a pencil and paper, and your fingers. They frown on applicants who need to remove their socks for this type of test (although you would probably be allowed to do this if you actually got the job). It's helpful to think out loud as you attempt the calculation, "Four plus ten equals seventeen, so carry the one, multiply by the number of days in the month, and divide by one hundred…" This way they can keep track of exactly how bad your maths skills are, and it will give them something to discuss in the canteen later. For maximum humiliation, it's best to employ this method when applying for another job with the same employer – that way the gossip about your embarrassing interview is bound to find its way back to your own office sooner or later, and all your colleagues can snigger at you.

Alternatively, it may be a computer skills test. It is worth remembering that every company will have its own unique computer set-up. Thus, no matter how familiar you are with your current employer's system, and no matter how confident you are that you will be able to navigate a similar system at interview, shortly after you sit down to begin your skills test, you will discover that you have been labouring under a particularly unfortunate misapprehension.

Alternatively, you will forget how to use a keyboard.

It's best to go in to these situations completely unprepared and then panic when they point you towards the computer. Here are a few suggestions to help you get through the computer skills test:

- Save your document to the wrong file.
- Delete your document.
- Delete one or two other documents they've inadvertently left on the hard drive.
- Try to do the spreadsheet using a ruler to draw out the lines.

Some interviewers will provide you with a list of questions prior to the interview, and will therefore expect you to arrive fully prepared to answer them. It is enormously helpful if you can manage one or more of the following:

- Mis-read the questions.
- Forget your notes.
- Forget your glasses.
- Read the same presentation you used for an interview last week.

It is sometimes suggested that if you feel intimidated you should try to imagine your audience with no clothes on. This is a tactic virtually guaranteed to cause humiliation. If the interview panel is made up of attractive members of the opposite sex, it is quite probable that you will begin drooling and find yourself unable to remember the question. If, on the other hand, the interviewers do not meet your own strict definition of the word "attractive", there is a distinct possibility that you will begin to giggle uncontrollably, and this is a behaviour which is unlikely to endear you to them.

Your first day

You will, naturally, arrive late. This is an obvious step and you should not need to be reminded of it.

Start by introducing yourself to your new colleagues, and tell them straight away about all your personal problems, including graphic details of your most recent visit to hospital/the dentist/the back seat of your partner's car. They can't fail to appreciate your openness and honesty.

Remember, you will have been given the job ahead of some long-standing and popular member of staff (employers like to do this – it's the only entertainment they get). This situation is not calculated to facilitate your immediate acceptance into the team, and can lay an important foundation towards your ultimate humiliation.

One quick way to speed your journey along the path to Total Humiliation is to have your partner, or some vague acquaintance, send you a strip-o-gram on your first day. This will ensure that all your new colleagues will know exactly who you are.

In addition, it will help enormously if you can bring yourself not to conform. Most people are basically conformists – they do pretty much what is expected of them pretty much when it's expected of them. It isn't easy to break free from the constraints of many years of social conditioning, but some people do manage – those who are clearly destined for Enlightenment and Total Humiliation. So, be prepared to take advantage of any opportunities to practise your new found non-conformity.

Here are some recommended activities for the aspiring non-conformist:

- Park your car in a non-designated space.
- Develop your own filing system using numerology and the position of the stars at the time a particular document is filed.
- Insist on working to New York time (or if you are in New York, use GMT).
- Shave off half of your moustache. The left half.

Once you have settled in

Senior management usually give advance notice of their visits. This is basically so that all the middle managers can whip themselves up into a nice state of panic. They will then go to extreme lengths to hide the harsh realities of everyday office life from senior management, who presumably have lived sheltered lives and not been exposed to such vulgarisms as coffee cups, personal effects, and tea ladies. You will soon learn to recognise the signs of an impending visit by Senior Management. You will arrive at work as usual (late!) to discover that someone has written spurious performance figures on large notice boards dotted around the office, and has conducted a thorough de-cluttering operation in the night. You will find all your paperwork dumped unceremoniously into your desk drawer, and your calendar featuring tasteful pictures of half-naked firemen will have mysteriously vanished. Here is what you should do when a member of Senior Management approaches your area of the office:

- Check your appearance, and attend to any little matters of personal hygiene such as cleaning out your ears.
- Allow them to find you doing the crossword/asleep/having sex.
- Allow them to see you trying to fix the photocopier. This is without doubt the most humiliating thing you can be caught doing. Photocopier manufacturers think their customers are idiots, so they give repair instructions in the form of pictures with flashing doors to show you which bit to open. Photocopier manufacturers are also sadists, and the pictures bear no relation to the actual fault. Within minutes you will be on the floor tearing your hair out and screaming incomprehensible curses. A more productive repair procedure can be employed with a large mallet.

It will also be helpful to familiarise yourself with the terminology used in modern businesses. Here are a few examples to start you off:

- Paperless office – you will not be allowed to read the Daily Mail at your desk.
- Means-end inversion – an advanced sexual position.
- Consumables – biscuits, sweets and cakes.
- Stationery cupboard – a cupboard that doesn't move very much.
- Mute button – what you press when you want to swear at the customer.
- Hold button – what you press when it's time for your tea break.
- Tea break – what you spend 90% of your day doing.
- Lunch break – 20 minutes when you're allowed out to see daylight.
- Internal directory – something to discuss with your gynaecologist.
- Time Management – a good game to try on Monday morning.
- Stress Management – a good game for Monday afternoon.
- Performance Targets – something you pin to a dart board.
- Performance Review – a list of everything you've done wrong in the last year.
- Clean Desk Policy – bring your own polish.
- Delegate – like a five-bar gate, but bigger.
- Team Building – being forced to spend the day doing pointless exercises with people you hate, with the end result that you hate them more than ever.

Should you find yourself elevated to the position of manager, you will have many opportunities for increasing your popularity by humiliating both yourself and your subordinates. You can try using quaint little nicknames, like "Oi", and shouting this term of endearment to them across the office. I once worked with a manager who called his secretary "Oi," and can confirm he was immensely popular.

Once you achieve management status, you will be required to conduct performance appraisals. Try putting low scores on the office notice board. Humiliating your subordinates in this way will facilitate their progress along the tortuous Path to Enlightenment, and can only enhance your reputation as the office diplomat. Conversely, try putting high scores in the team newsletter – this will elevate the staff member concerned to the status of "teacher's pet", which is sure to make them popular.

Another jolly wheeze is to rearrange the desks over the weekend. Your employees will surely be thrilled to return to work on Monday and find that their window seat has been replaced by a view of the toilets. When your own manager finds out who is to blame for the resulting strike, you are sure to be rewarded with a very public humiliation.

Work social events
There are those events which purport to be purely social, although any comments made to your manager in the relaxed setting of the local pub will nonetheless be remembered and noted on your annual performance appraisal. It will also be noted if you and one or more of your colleagues spend too long in the toilets together and how much alcohol you consume, and this sort of thing is likely to find its way into the staff newsletter.

Then there are those events which are laughingly referred to as "training courses". One exercise, popular some years ago on local authority training courses is the "melted cheese" game. In this, one person is the toast, and the other person has to lie on top of them and pretend to be the cheese melting. History can only guess at the perceived benefit of this team-building exercise, but it has been suggested that the enlightened humiliation resulting from this exercise could be fruitfully enhanced by videotaping it and playing it back at the office party.

Many organisations now promote out-of-hours team-building sessions where you can build rapport with your colleagues without actually using up any work time, and usually without costing the company a penny (the time lost in hangovers the next day doesn't count).

Such events might be activity-based, such as ten-pin bowling, where you get to show off your ineptitude in a completely different field. Alternatively, the event may be more traditional, such as a visit to a tasteful hostelry where strange-coloured liquid can be consumed in a pleasant atmosphere, and you can indulge in a friendly altercation with your immediate supervisor, safe in the knowledge that he will have forgotten all about it in the morning (you will be wrong, of course). You will mark your territory by spilling a drink, and then guard your seat fiercely until you finally fall off it. At this point you can sit cross-legged on the floor and begin to chant "Om...Om...Om..." This will ensure that your colleagues see you as the idiot you truly are.

For enhanced humiliation do take your partner along to the works night out. He/she will be presented with an unrivalled opportunity to talk face to face with your colleagues, and there's no telling what kind of personal information they may be swapping about you.

Alternatively, your partner will sit in a corner and refuse to talk to anyone. This behaviour will mark your partner out as a miserable loser, and the accompanying glory will be reflected back to you.

Of course, team building does not have to be a specific event. The Seeker on the Path will endeavour to build rapport with colleagues on a daily basis. Here are some suggestions:

- Bring in your holiday photos, forgetting to remove the ones of you sunbathing nude, and dribbling into your tequila sunrise.
- Point out to a female colleague that her thong is showing.
- Point out to a male colleague that his thong is showing.
- Buy a well-known anti-dandruff shampoo as a birthday gift for your manager.
- Talk about personal freshness, and reach for your gas mask.

Your annual appraisal

Your pay rise will depend on this, so it's important to be prepared. You might like to make a list of all your mistakes, errors of judgement and general cock-ups in advance of the actual appraisal. Then, jump in first with your explanations and apologies. You may consider this a clever pre-emptive strike to prove to your manager that you are aware of your failings, and are eager to improve. Unfortunately, it is more likely that you have just told your boss a dozen things you did wrong that she either didn't know about, or knew about but thought were down to someone else. Once you realise this, you will begin to feel supremely humble; and you will have taken another important step along the Great Path. Remember then, your annual performance appraisal, if handled appropriately, can represent an unparalleled opportunity for spiritual growth.

Chapter 2
Relationships

*Weddings provide a number of opportunities
for mass humiliation, as just about anyone involved
can manage to do something stupid.*

Inspiration
- Gentle persuasion or encouragement will get you a lot further than demanding or pleading. This may be true when it comes to sex, but it doesn't apply to housework.
- Honesty is the best policy. Unless you've done something totally bloody stupid, in which case lying through your teeth is recommended.
- In the field of humiliation, it's not so much what you do, as who you do it to.
- *Why* you do something for your partner is more important than *what* you do. Thus, if your partner has asked you to do the ironing and you inadvertently burn a hole through an expensive item of clothing because you were engrossed in Match of the Day, this will be okay. The important thing is that you did the ironing specifically because your partner had asked you to.
- A friend in need... can really get on your nerves.

Application

- Don't invite a vegetarian to a carvery for your first date. This is something best left until the relationship has had time to sour.
- Always keep your promises. Well nearly always. Well, the important ones anyway.
- Your spouse likes consistency. Try to always be a prat.
- Own your relationship. Sadly, this doesn't mean you can get a refund.
- Never give your real name.
- Don't get caught.
- Always remember everything your partner does wrong.

Dating

There are many different opportunities for humiliation when dating. You can start by identifying some likely looking beau or belle across the room. Stare at him (or her), then smile and look away coyly when they notice. Know when to stop or you could find yourself accused of stalking. Smile seductively. If self-humiliation is your goal, it's always better to have eaten something immediately prior to the smiling – spinach is very good for attaching itself to the teeth, and remaining there all evening until you look in a mirror.

Saunter over, preferably tripping yourself up en route, and employ an original opening line. "Do you come here often?" rarely fails to raise a laugh, and "Get your coat, you've pulled!" is pretty good for eliciting an unanticipated physical response, although it should be noted that this is more likely to predispose you to unconsciousness than enlightenment.

Now you are ready for the next stage of dating humiliation. Start by spilling your drink and follow up with kissing absolutely everyone and declaring your undying love for the next person to buy you a drink. If your chosen venue has a live band playing, so much the better. Feel free to jump on stage and join them – they love it when members of the public take a genuine interest.

You are now ready for the final stage of dating humiliation, although if you have been following the instructions closely you will be far too drunk to feel at all humiliated until your friends tell you about it the next day. Retire to the toilets and then pass out in the cubicle. Have a friend with you, who doesn't mind climbing over toilet doors to facilitate your escape, and who will accompany you to the hospital, where student doctors will snigger at you.

For men, your body mass apparently means that you can hold your booze better than the ladies, so you probably won't need to go to such extremes to humiliate yourself. It should be sufficient to drink until you throw up, and then leap onto the table and begin to strip.

Perhaps you feel more comfortable meeting new people in other environments. Here are a few suggestions:

Martial arts classes are a nice informal way of meeting people and collecting bruises at the same time. You have no chance whatsoever of looking suave and sophisticated when being thrown to the floor repeatedly; and try flirting when you are in traction.

Many supermarkets now hold singles evenings, where unattached people can meet while doing their grocery shopping. Do have some intimate, personal items in your basket; this will provide a useful talking point (such as, what do you intend doing with a bunch of bananas, some whipped cream and a pack of AA batteries?). As you head for the checkout, you will realise that you have left your purse/wallet at home, and your new-found friend will no doubt be very impressed as you try to explain this to the checkout operator.

Many people meet their partners at work, and it gives an ideal opportunity to demonstrate to a prospective partner on a daily basis just how sexy and suave you are not. To spread out the humiliation over the longest possible period, do tell your colleagues as soon as you develop a crush on someone at work. Swear them to secrecy, but don't be surprised when it appears in the office newsletter by Thursday.

The office party will provide an excellent opportunity to casually introduce yourself to the person you are interested in, but there are some important things you must do to prepare yourself for this moment. First, ensure that you have not eaten all day so that when you begin to partake of the punch it will be the first thing to hit your stomach, and will therefore be significantly more potent. Chat to your friends, all the time, throwing seductive glances at your prey (who will probably think you have indigestion). Continue to partake of the punch. If you have planned this carefully, you will have cunningly made your way around the office and will be just about to introduce yourself to your chosen prey when the combined effects of the punch and the lack of food will kick in, and you will slowly fall to the floor in a crumpled and humiliated heap. The most powerful memory the man or woman of your dreams will have of you, will be the sight of your colleagues scooping you up into a wheelchair and ferrying you off to the loo.

You might like to try humiliating your friends by fixing them up with blind dates. Unintentional humiliation is so much more effective than overt mischief-making. This way, because everyone knows that you meant well, your friends will feel obliged to sit through the entire evening with someone who talks too loudly, complains too much about the food, the service and the decor, or simply spends the entire time rambling on about his or her ex.

There is a school of thought which maintains that once a relationship ends you need some kind of emotional closure to enable you to move on with your life. Emotional closure would be defined as a dignified gesture, such as returning all your ex's belongings. Dignified, but strangely unsatisfying.

For genuine closure it is suggested that you try revenge. There is no better way to mark the end of a relationship, and this is also an extremely useful tactic to aid your progress on the Path.

You might arrange some tortuous humiliation for your ex, such as giving away all their secrets/clothes/CDs/diaries. If handled with care, you can humiliate yourself as well, and any of your friends who happen to be present, when you embark on some petty display of retribution, such as walking up to your ex in a restaurant with his new partner, and pouring a plate of spaghetti bolognaise over his head.

The wedding

Many people nowadays avoid this step altogether and go straight onto living together. In doing so they are bypassing one of life's most promising ways to humiliate themselves. In addition, it could be argued, they are damaging the long-term stability of their relationship. Going through a traumatic event is known to bring couples closer together, and what can be more traumatic than standing in front of your friends, family, and people you were forced to invite because they used to baby-sit for you, and getting your marriage vows totally wrong? This kind of joint humiliation is bound to cement any relationship.

Before the ceremony, nerves being what they are, it can be all too easy to find you have suddenly forgotten how to walk. You will have to be helped up the aisle by a small child carrying a bouquet of flowers and a concealed personal stereo. The child will, of course, be the son or daughter of a close relative, and will (apparently) be doing a sterling job as page boy or bridesmaid; and the rest of the congregation will fail to notice any inappropriate behaviour until the earpiece falls out and you find yourself giving your vows to the accompaniment of Gareth Gates' latest release.

After the ceremony your nerves should have calmed significantly and you will be able to get to the bar. This is the point at which your friends and relatives will come together in a ritual punch-up to settle old gripes, and score a few points for themselves on the humiliation-o-meter. Once the police have left you can get on with enjoying the party.

Any unattached young men at the wedding will consider this the ideal opportunity to remove their clothing as they dance. Anthropologists have yet to establish the evolutionary benefits of this ritual, other than having the effect of speedily removing all your prim maiden aunts from the room.

Weddings provide a number of opportunities for mass humiliation, as just about anyone involved can manage to do something stupid. The Best Man, for example, will give a ribald speech about the exploits of the groom in his younger days, and will round off by getting the bride's name wrong; and later will be caught underneath the head table with the Chief Bridesmaid.

The bridesmaids, in their turn, will decorate the wrong car with shaving foam and tin cans; and will sing a variety of extremely rude songs before they realise the whole thing is being video-taped.

Humiliation need not be restricted to members of the wedding party, though. Even as a guest you can humiliate yourself and your dear friend the bride/groom by engaging in a quiet chat with their new mother-in-law about how you thought they'd never settle down, what with all that history of one-night stands/gambling debts, and that brief stay at Her Majesty's pleasure.

Sex
This hardly needs to be explained – the whole thing is specifically designed to humiliate. It's best done with the lights on so your partner can fully appreciate the look on your face when you first see him/her naked. You can help your partner's ego no end by rehearsing a few choice phrases and using them at appropriate moments. Do ensure your tone of voice carries no conviction whatsoever when you utter the words, "No, of course that wasn't too quick," or "Don't worry, it happens to all men at some time or another."

Here are some technical terms that you may wish to familiarise yourself with before you embark on a physical relationship:
- Oral sex – talking about it.
- Oral contraception – refusing to talk about it.
- 69 – what you get if you multiply six by eleven and a half. Honest.
- Orgasm – the art of making paper napkins into the shape of swans.
- Multiple orgasm – eating more than one chocolate bar.
- Dildo – a wooden rail which is sometimes fixed horizontally on

the walls, usually with floral wallpaper above it, and a plain paper below – this should tastefully pick out one of the colours used in the paper above.

Pregnancy and birth

Once you've mastered sexual humiliation in the bedroom, kitchen, car and office, you will be ready to move on to the more advanced level of humiliation that comes with pregnancy.

As a woman, this is probably the single most humiliating thing that will happen to you in your entire life. Dignity doesn't exist for pregnant women. Doctors take an unhealthy interest in your urine all of a sudden, and you will have to take jars of the stuff to your local GP every couple of weeks (he's probably selling it to private patients who think it will make them thin if they have it injected). You will also be subjected to weekly examinations where simply shaving your legs below the knee is not enough to maintain self-respect. Your doctor will make comments like "I wouldn't expect to feel the baby yet, *even in a thin person*," or "Open wide." A real barrel of laughs, and frankly you don't need to put any effort at all into humiliating yourself. This burden is taken from you by the medical profession.

In hospital you will be subjected to the kind of examinations and tortures that are outlawed under the Geneva Convention. Student doctors will crowd around your bed while your legs are held aloft in stirrups, and make private jokes to one another.

Midwives will tell you that you are not in enough pain to require drugs, and when you eventually do get some drugs it will be a duff batch. This is usually a good time to tell them that you've changed your mind and don't want to have a baby after all. You can try to escape, but you probably won't make it past the nurses' station, where they drink tea, eat biscuits, and act as catchers.

Do not be fooled into thinking the humiliation that comes with pregnancy is limited to the woman who is pregnant. If you are the father you will be required to go shopping for nipple cream, nursing bras, and disposable knickers. Your beloved, who was once a stable and reasonable person with whom you shared many common interests, will transform into a crazed despot who will yell at you in public for no apparent reason. And this is before the onset of labour.

Once admitted to hospital your role will be to sneak extra rations of food in for your partner.

Nowadays it is expected that you will be present at the birth. Do take along a camera or camcorder so you can capture the event, and don't hesitate to ask people to do it again if you miss that perfect shot. Remember, no amount of horror movies can prepare you for the trauma of watching your partner give birth for the first time. Do make sure your camera is in some kind of protective case so it doesn't get too badly damaged when you black out.

Men are from Snickers (like Mars but fifty per cent nuts)
Once upon a time it wasn't politically correct to think that there were any differences between men and women – they had to be treated equally in all things. Nowadays, people show how politically correct they are by telling you that men's and women's brains work differently. So it isn't sexist at all to expect a woman to do all the housework as long as the man can read a map. Believe this, and your spouse will take full advantage of any and every opportunity to humiliate you, thus saving you the trouble of doing it yourself.

Relationships change as they progress. Where once you would do anything to be together, now you will do anything to get out from under each other's feet. Possession of the TV remote is paramount, and you will take it with you whenever you get up for a cup of tea, lest your partner surreptitiously switches over to the snooker final/Coronation Street/Teletubbies while your back is turned.

They say that you should respect each other as you grow, and promote your partner's self-esteem even when you might want to be critical. It is vital that you do not speak out if your partner is about to do something ridiculous. Remember, you are facilitating their progress on the Path. Hence, if they can't sing a note, but have a burning desire to try karaoke, do encourage them, and ensure all their friends are there to watch.

Another good way to humiliate your partner is to flirt shamelessly in front of them. Even if your partner is not the jealous type, and knows that you are simply enjoying a bit of harmless fun, the sense of pity emanating from any onlookers will wash over your partner in waves of gradually deepening humiliation.

Chapter 3
Children

Your child will tell the entire school how much you earn and what Daddy does with his toenail clippings.

Inspiration
- Sleep is for wimps.
- Question not if the nappy is half-full or half-empty. Just get rid of it quickly.
- Requesting or encouraging will get you precisely nowhere.
- Think... plan... act... screw up.
- There is a right way and a wrong way. Choose the latter.
- What goes in determines what comes out. This applies particularly to nappies.
- If you are not making mistakes, you are asleep.
- You can achieve a lot with a little, if that little is totally inept.

Application
- There is no later. Do it now. This especially applies to feeding time.
- Schedule in time for your nervous breakdown.
- Always reward positive behaviour. Ignore negative behaviour. This may not be easy in a crowded supermarket but no-one ever said being a parent wasn't going to be fun.

- Never stop.
- Your child likes consistency. Try to always be an idiot.
- Own your relationship with your child. Remember, it's *your* fault.
- Throw the rule book out of the window – but make sure you have insurance in case it lands on someone.
- Be positive. Repeat after me, "I'm positive I can't cope."

Pre-school

Once upon a time you had a proper job and people listened to what you had to say. For women, this will have changed the minute you announced you were pregnant. This is the point, identified by medical professionals, at which you become not so much a person, as a suitcase.

It no longer matters if you have the ability to calculate the square root of minus one in your head and have a degree in astrophysics. From now on people will smile benevolently at you as they dismiss you. They will talk to your bump, and assume that you think of nothing but nipple cream and stretch marks. Try getting a refund of bank charges from your bank manager when you are pregnant. You may win, but it will be a pity win, and doesn't really count. You will have taken another important step on the route to Total Humiliation; and now you can look forward to the myriad joys of stress incontinence and perineal pain.

It takes a little longer for the effects of parenthood to be seen in men, but once you start turning up late and bleary-eyed for meetings, with unidentified stains on your shirt, you will have made significant progress on the Path. People will suddenly seem far less interested in what you have to say. You could tell them there's a mad axe murderer in the conference room, or even a company auditor, and people will simply assume these are the delusional ravings of a sleep-deprived idiot.

Sleep deprivation is a vital tool. They apparently use it for brainwashing in strange religious cults, though no-one knows for sure if they got the idea from babies. In religious cults you come out muttering about the spiritual implications of shaving your head, wearing orange clothes, and giving away all your money. With babies, it's the same principle, but you come out muttering about Teletubbies.

Your baby will project strange substances onto your clothes (from both ends) and you will remain completely oblivious to the presence of these stains until you stand up in front of the entire office to give a presentation to the Managing Director. Do endeavour to carry a bag of spare nappies with you, even if you have left the baby at nursery. The presence of nappies in an office setting is somewhat incongruous, and will represent a valuable addition to your briefcase.

Do not underestimate the value of nappies in speeding your journey on the Path. Look for original ways to dispose of them, for example. Most people, somewhat conventionally, tie them up in a fragranced nappy sack and stash them in the bin. How about flushing them? This will cause almost instantaneous humiliation if you try it in a public place such as a restaurant – they tend to have rather odd ideas about customers blocking the toilets with nappies and flooding the floor. The posher the restaurant, the greater the likelihood of extreme humiliation.

Alternatively, at home, you could try wrapping the nappy up in that jolly little nappy sack and then just drop it out of the bathroom window. You will maintain that the intention is to collect them up and put them straight in the outside bin, and therefore save time traipsing through the house to the bin every time your little one does a wee. However, it is only a matter of time before you drop the nappy sack out of the window, only to have it land squarely on the head of some poor bloke who's come to read the meter.

One day (one will probably be sufficient) you will take your newborn to the office to proudly show him off to your colleagues. They will gather round eagerly, not so much because they love babies, but because it's an excuse to avoid work for a few minutes. Your boss will, naturally, hate children, but will be unable to resist when you thrust the baby into his/her arms while you rummage around your bag for a spare nappy and some nappy rash cream. The baby will then throw up on your boss, and you will never be viewed in quite the same light again.

It is vitally important, they say, to breastfeed. The opportunities for humiliation in this area are many and varied. Try lobbing out your boobs in front of your husband's friends. They may all have secretly wanted to see you naked in the past, but with a baby attached to your nipple, it's just not the same. You can clear a room of hard-drinking rugby players in minutes using this method, and they will never be able to look you in the eye again.

You will, naturally, want to take your offspring with you everywhere. Seekers on the Path know all too well the power of a toddler for humiliating its parents. In restaurants, they will scream and run about stealing serviettes and small items of cutlery from the other tables. In shops they will scream and lie on the floor kicking and thumping because you dared utter the forbidden word, "no".

At playgroups they will scream, and your child will be the only one who won't join in with any of the organised activities, who elbows all the other children out of the ball pit, and who then forgets how to use a potty.

School
Once your child starts school you may think that this signals your return to a normal life. Do not be fooled. You now have to contend with primary school teachers who are so accustomed to speaking to four-year-olds, that this spills over into their dealings with you, and no amount of power dressing will change this. Your child will tell the entire school how much you earn and what Daddy does with his toenail clippings.

Once it has been established through the comments of your children that you are not as rich/cool/clever/sophisticated as all the other parents, it is time to move on to impressing the other parents directly. This is best tackled in the playground. When you drop little Torquil off at school, do make that extra bit of effort to be late. It's the little things that count, and this small point will make all the difference. The other parents will, of course, be leaving by the time you arrive, but you will still have time to notice that they are all smartly dressed and calm as they head off for the office. There is always one parent who arrives late, half-dressed with wet hair and no make-up. Let it be you.

Notice, also, that the other parents, as they head off to work, are doing so in shiny, expensive, new cars. Do not allow yourself to be swayed by this, such material possessions are unnecessary for seekers of True Enlightenment. Invest instead, in a rusty old car, preferably with at least one door in a contrasting colour where someone has botched up a repair job. If you must insist on having the shiny new BMW, please remember the fluffy dice. This will go some way to mitigating the effects.

Next you can move on to conversations in the playground while you wait for your little darlings to be released at the end of the day. Here you will find that all the other parents have more qualifications and better jobs than you. Do not be intimidated; simply ensure that you get everyone's name wrong. The surest path to humiliation is to boast about something that is completely unimpressive, or just say something really stupid with conviction. Here are a few throwaway lines you could try:

- My other car is a Hillman Imp.
- I have a lovely collection of garden gnomes.
- I must buy some haemorrhoid cream.
- I had one of those once but it got repossessed.

This is just everyday school life. The real fun starts with the school play, where your child will start a punch up in the choir.

Other school events should also be attended. Here are some possibilities:

- Fashion Show – your child should be the one who forgets his underpants.
- Bring and Buy Sale – show off your lack of talent at baking cakes for the sale.
- Quiz Night – see how many questions you can get wrong.
- Talent Show – sing Patricia The Stripper, with feeling.

Entertaining their friends

You can do this simply by falling over in the playground, or by having an argument with one of the teachers. If you are feeling more adventurous, however, you could invite your child's friends round for tea.

You should, of course, have spent many years in preparation and will have a wealth of experience at burning. It is possible, with practice, to burn the outside skin of a sausage to charcoal, while leaving the insides utterly raw and inedible. You can do the same sort of thing with chicken nuggets, chips, pasties, fish fingers, pizza... in fact, with a little imagination the possibilities are limitless. Vegetables should be left to boil over, thus flooding the top of the cooker. Careful positioning of the smoke alarm will ensure that this is triggered, which can only add to the general fun. The sound of your screams and curses as you try to clean up the mess and salvage what you can will probably haunt little Torquil and his friends for years. If you can arrange for the cat to bring home a half-eaten mouse and tear through the house with it at this stage, it will only enhance your progress on the Path.

Remember that inviting school-friends round for tea means that their parents will want to come and collect them. You will have to invite them in, and you should ensure that the house is a complete tip, and that you have two or three unfinished decorating jobs on the go.

Birthday parties

For maximum humiliation you should consider holding the party at home. There are many books on the market which offer excellent advice on how to raise children, run a home and hold down a job, all while also retaining your sanity. Remember, these books do not apply to you.

Real parents do not live ordered, organised lives. They live hectic, sleepless, chaotic lives, lurching helplessly from one pile of ironing to the next. Hence, the ordeal of holding your children's party at home will have a similar humiliating effect to inviting their friends round for tea, but on a much grander scale.

No matter how hard you try to present the image of perfect family life, by tidying the kitchen and lounge where you will be entertaining your guests, the children will nonetheless find their way into the bedrooms where you thought you had hidden away all your clutter.

You may prefer the safer option of one of those child-friendly restaurants where they allegedly do everything for you. At least you don't have to tidy your house for this, but you are expected to arrive before your guests. An excellent technique, then, is to turn up late, to be greeted by a row of all your child's friends (and their parents), waiting impatiently for your arrival. At least you get to make an entrance.

Another good ploy is to invite slightly more people than the restaurant is able to cater for. We're not talking about anything of biblical proportions, but say the maximum number is twenty-two. You're pretty safe if you invite twenty-five because you can guarantee some of the people won't be able to come. The fatal flaw in this plan, of course, is that if you count on them not turning up, it's absolutely guaranteed that they will. You will now have to explain your situation to the restaurant employees who, despite working in a restaurant, will tell you that they do not know how to cater for two extra people.

They may not actually suggest that you turn away the extras, but the thought will be left hanging in the air.

There are some basic steps to follow for children's parties. First, do let your child hand out the invitations himself. This way, roughly 90% of the invitations will never make it home, but will instead disappear into the mysterious Cloakroom Triangle (like the one in Bermuda, but strangely limited to a very specific area of the school classroom). Hence, the day before the party will dawn and you will not have received any replies to the invitations. You will then have to make a series of frantic and apologetic telephone calls to alert the other parents to the impending party, and this is the kind of event that will become legendary in the playground. You will truly be elevated to the status of imbecile.

For added effect and further humiliation you could also defer to your five-year-old's judgement when he says he wants to invite the whole class to his party except for Tom and Joanna. This way you have to be extremely furtive when approaching parents in the playground to ask if their little one will be attending, so that you don't offend the parents of those not invited. Do not worry, the more furtive you are, the more you will draw attention to yourself. The parents of Tom and Joanna will undoubtedly find out, and so will everyone else, who will think you're petty and mean for not inviting these two little angels.

Next, try forgetting the names of your children's friends – this is especially helpful when talking to their respective parents.

On the day of the party, if there is a bouncy castle or a slide, do join in – there is little that can top a trip to casualty for utter humiliation. Especially when you have to explain to the assembled student doctors that the sprained ankle was sustained in a pitched battle to out-bounce a five-year-old.

Pantomime

Nowhere do the words "children" and "humiliation" go together better than in the sphere of pantomime. You can start off by irritating the box office assistant. Be indecisive about which performance you wish to attend, and where you would like to sit. Next, make a decision, but don't stick to it. Tell them you'll ring back later when you've had time to think about it. If you wait long enough, the seats you wanted will have been sold to someone else and you'll have to start the process all over again. The act of being indecisive on a daily basis in the presence of a box office assistant is excruciatingly embarrassing, and sets the scene for the Total Humiliation you will doubtless endure on the day of the performance.

On the day itself, do remember the basics and make sure you are running late. The car park will be full so you will wind up in some little back alley miles from civilization where tossing the hubcaps of visiting cars is a local pastime.

Leap out of the car in all your finery and hurry off towards the theatre, making sure to keep your tickets in a safe place. Leave the children to pound mercilessly on the theatre doors (which will have closed by this time) while you rush back to the car for the tickets. This will guarantee a warm reception from the theatre manager.

You will have missed all the boring stuff at the start while other people's children climb over three rows of seats to pick a fight with someone they know from school, while waiting for the show to start. This is no bad thing. You will also have missed the lights going down, the curtain going up, and the first seven minutes of the show. This means that you are clearly visible to those on stage as you make your way cautiously to your seat, and they will feel obliged to make you the butt of their jokes.

For maximum humiliation it is best to sit in the stalls, fairly close to the front. Anywhere in the first eight or nine rows will leave you nicely within firing range when they start squirting water at the audience, and also means you are conveniently placed when they start asking for volunteers. This is where your child will demonstrate superhuman strength and thrust your arm in the air before your brain has had time to fully comprehend the question. A spotlight will settle on you, and helpful members of the cast will rush over to guide you to the stage. Tripping up will again prove a useful part of your repertoire. Once on stage you will be visible to the entire audience, and now you will appreciate all that time spent in choosing attire which does not co-ordinate with anything.

You will, naturally, be unshaven if you are a man while thin, floaty, dresses which become transparent when backlit are recommended for women.

Being the centre of attention in this very specialised arena is humiliating in itself. If they ask you to remove your glasses, and present you with a plastic bag to cover your clothes with, well you're onto a winner in the humiliation stakes. You will not be allowed back to your seat and the loving arms of your children (don't forget who got you into this mess in the first place) before you have taken at least one custard pie in the face.

Chapter 4
Recreation and Leisure

The inability to cook even the simplest of meals will allow you an unequalled opportunity for humiliation at least once every single day.

Inspiration

- You can do a little with a lot, if you plan it right.
- A needle in a haystack will nonetheless prick your finger.
- A creative mind may very well survive poor training, but there's no substitute for active humiliation.
- It is better to humiliate yourself magnificently than merely to get through the day.
- The man who never made mistakes, never was humiliated.
- All work and no play... will severely restrict your opportunities for humiliation.
- The only thing holding you back is yourself. And the neighbours, who've threatened to call the police if you don't keep the noise down.
- Think of your hobby as your reward for screwing up your working life.
- When you score a maximum break in snooker, it will always be in a practice session.

Application

- Do your very best at each stage of the game. Or simply cheat.
- Develop as wide a range of interests as possible – that way you can be inept in many different fields.
- If you seem to be running fast but getting nowhere, you're probably at the gym.
- Make a habit of being inept.
- Always be on the lookout for new things you can fail at.
- Always cheat.

This chapter covers that part of our lives over which we allegedly have the most control – our leisure time. Here, we will discuss how choosing the right hobbies and activities can help us to maximise the opportunities for humiliation.

DIY

An endlessly inventive way of spending money you don't have on power tools that will be used once, and then left to rust in the garage. You will, of course, tell all your friends how good you are at DIY, and they will believe you... until they ask you to repair a leaking tap and you flood the bathroom floor instead.

Similarly, when you have spent many hours talking to your friends about DIY until they become convinced that you are competent in this field, they will volunteer your services to help out their other friends. Thus, when you lay kitchen lino for a friend of a friend, and it ends up looking like bubble wrap, the humiliation will spread not just to yourself, but to the friend who recommended you. If you do have the inclination to attempt a bit of DIY, there are some important things you can do to increase the humiliation factor. For example, you should *always* assume you are good enough to Do-It-Yourself, whether it's bleeding a radiator, or tackling a full-scale loft conversion. If you don't have the right tools, use whatever you have to hand. This might mean that you end up fitting a carpet with a hammer and nails, but at least you can show off your handiwork to all your friends and tell them proudly that you did it all by yourself.

Golf

Golfers wear the sort of clothes that normal people would only wear for a bet. If you can infiltrate this exclusive society you can find out where they shop and join them.

On a more serious note, it is a well known fact that many big business deals are conducted, not in the conference room, but on the golf course. Should your manager see any spark of potential in you he may invite you along to join him at such a meeting. Naturally you will tell him that you have played before. Remember, this could be important to your career.

You may get away with missing the ball and spending 80% of the day in a bunker; since this could be put down to simple bad luck. But your manager, having recommended you to join this elite squad, will not appreciate it if, in your eagerness to impress, you continually talk when people are trying to take a shot.

He will be equally unimpressed if you beat him.

Keeping fit

Seek out one of those ridiculously expensive gyms, where you will have to exercise alongside slim, attractive people in designer clothes.

Your baggy T-shirt and leggings will secure your place in the social hierarchy, and then to further your progress on the Path you can fall off the jogging machine, which will be conveniently placed in full view of your friends, relaxing in the cafe. Remember that your friends will all be fitter than you, and will be able to jog for half an hour without so much as a single bead of sweat gracing their foreheads. You, on the other hand, will look and feel like you have just crawled out of a sewer. This will be especially noticeable if you have agreed to a quick game of football in your lunch break. You will have to return to work, red-faced, sweating, and unable to walk properly for the rest of the day. You will, naturally, check that the coast is clear but it is nevertheless guaranteed that someone will walk past every time you decide to risk smelling your own armpit.

Eating out
You will be instantly popular with the chef if you keep sending the waitress in to check on ingredients, so it can be terribly helpful to be a picky eater. Convert to one of those religions that only allows you to eat chips cooked in a specific type of vegetable oil (and then only on a Tuesday), or even better, become a vegetarian. That way you can insist that they read you the entire list of ingredients, and you can engage the chef in a public debate on the legal definition of the word "vegetarian".

It's immensely helpful to take your children with you when eating out. If you have schooled them well they will sit quietly and make polite conversation for about thirty seconds – after that they will be off to the kitchens to find something more interesting to do. They will run in between the tables playing tag, and gather up all the little sachets of sauce, and proceed to throw them at each other. They will also eat their food with their fingers – this may be acceptable with sandwiches, but people will look at you strangely if they try it with curry and rice.

You might simply accept that dining at a smart and sophisticated venue is something that will not apply to you for the next sixteen years or so; and go to one of those nice child-friendly restaurants instead. These provide some excellent opportunities for humiliation. Your children will, of course, still run around joyously, but it will not be quite so noticeable because everyone else's children will be doing exactly the same thing. You have to use your imagination a little more in order to humiliate yourself in this setting, but with skill it can be done.

It is recommended that you join the children in a game of tag, and do go down the slide at least twice. This is a popular activity amongst mothers, although many disguise their enthusiasm with excuses that they were only there to rescue their child who had climbed too high and got scared.

Shopping

Do not carry cash. This way you can hold up an entire queue of people by paying for your daily newspaper with a cheque. You can also try this technique at an ice-cream van – it will do wonders for your image.

When out shopping, never accept the first item they show you. Shoes, for example, are unique items – you may be presented with two pairs of the same size and style, but this does not mean that they are identical. The cobbler (it is important to use the correct terminology when buying shoes. Remember this – the shop assistant will respect you for it) may have been having a bad day when he made one of the shoes, and you will not know unless you try on each and every shoe. Walk up and down. Ask the shop assistant what he/she thinks. Ask any passing shoppers for their opinions. Phone a friend and ask them. Now decide to go and think about it over a nice cup of tea and a muffin. Go back once you are refreshed and ask to see the same shoe in a different colour. The shop assistant will be delighted to see you.

It's much easier to humiliate yourself in a clothes shop. Do walk out into the main shop area when trying on a new outfit, especially if you are in denial about your clothes size. It is particularly beneficial to try on anything with a zip, in order to take full advantage of the horrors that ensue when it gets stuck.

Here are some tips for men, forced to go shopping with (or for) your partners. These are tried and tested methods for humiliating yourself and/or your partner. Use them with care.

If your partner asks your opinion of a lingerie item, reply loudly, "It all looks the same on the bedroom floor".

Buy lingerie for your loved one. If you have no idea what size your partner is you can look around for a similar-sized shop assistant to embarrass. Now cup your hands to demonstrate bust size. You will inevitably wind up buying something the wrong size, and whether it's too big or too small, you lose because your partner will manage to see an insult either way.

You should give some thought to whom you go shopping with. The whole event is much more fun with a friend or partner, and you can take turns to embarrass each other. Women, for example, tend to be uncomfortable if you discuss their dress size in anything more than a whisper. When your friend has tried on the first outfit and found it too tight, it will be your job to scour the clothes rails for the next size up whilst doing nothing so crass as actually telling the shop assistant what size you are looking for.

You might also embarrass your friend by leaning against the shop doorway with an expression of terminal boredom while she tries on almost everything in the store.

Sticking with sweeping generalisations, the tables are turned when the male of the species enters a DIY store. Now the female partner gets to stand around looking bored, and telling the shop assistants that she doesn't know who her partner is trying to kid because he's so utterly useless at DIY. Of course, there are a growing number of female DIY enthusiasts, but their presence in a DIY store is more likely to embarrass the shop assistant, who will initially assume that they don't know what they are talking about and will patronise them mercilessly.

Car boot sales
Always assume that the seller doesn't know what he has got, and that you can buy it cheap and sell at a profit. You will be wrong 100% of the time. The seller always knows what he has got – it is his job to fool you into thinking he doesn't, so that you will buy it at a grossly inflated price, and therefore end up being completely humiliated when you find out you've just paid £10 for a vase that costs £2.50 in the shops.

Auctions
You will get carried away in a bidding war with a little old dear (who is probably a plant) and have to sneak out of the auction room before they get your name. Alternatively you will find you have been inadvertently bidding against your partner on the other side of the room.

You are less likely to encounter such problems when using Internet auction sites, but you will still get carried away and end up bidding more than the item would cost you to buy in the shops. Then you will have to pay postage as well. This is an excellent example of how to humiliate yourself in the privacy of your own home.

Swimming
You've spent months hiding your cellulite/beer belly under baggy jumpers. Now is the time to expose all that flab and unwanted body hair to the public at large. Oh, and if you forget how to swim, this can only speed your progress on the Path. There isn't much that is more humiliating than having to be rescued from the shallow end by the local authority lifeguard.

Other sporting activities
For many of us, regular exercise is more of an aspiration than a reality. It is, therefore, incredibly easy to humiliate ourselves in just about any sporting arena. If you have no co-ordination, you should be particularly inept at Kung Fu, for example. The moves look smooth and effortless when demonstrated by the instructor, but once it's your turn to try you will suddenly discover that you don't have enough arms to block the attack, and will flail around uselessly like a jellyfish.

If there is any sporting activity that you are actually good at, you might humiliate your friends by simply beating them time after time. This might be considered rude, however, and for a more genuine, loving, humiliation I would recommend that you accompany your friend whenever he or she is taking part in an activity. Now, all you need do is be incredibly over-enthusiastic in your support. Cheering every time your friend pots a ball in snooker is sure to be well received.

This approach also works well if your friend is horse riding. The sudden noise may upset the horse and lead to your friend coming into unexpected contact with the ground.

Cooking and baking

As has been mentioned before, cooking is a specialised skill. The inability to cook even the simplest of meals will allow you an unequalled opportunity for humiliation at least once every single day. For increased humiliation, though, try inviting people round for a dinner party. It's important to invite people who either don't like you very much (in-laws are a good choice) or people you need to impress (your boss, for example). Now, don't bother with basic things like egg and chips – any idiot can get that wrong. Go for the jackpot and try something really adventurous in the hope that your friends and family will finally see you as a talented chef with skills to rival Jamie Oliver.

Do keep the telephone number of the local Chinese Takeaway handy for when it all goes horribly wrong.

Conversely, if you are a guest at a friend's dinner party, you might try spreading the humiliation their way by politely enthusing about the food, but then sneaking most of it to the dog under the table.

Protests

This was a terribly popular hobby back in the 1980s and like flares and platform shoes, it is due for a comeback. It doesn't really matter what you protest about; it's the act of protesting that counts. A crowd of people marching along the street with banners held high will always attract attention, but for increased humiliation value, you should try doing it alone. Chanting would be an effective tool to employ.

You may also like to try protesting within your local shops. The scope for humiliation is usually limited to the one or two shop assistants who aren't actually on their tea break, but you could improve on this by informing the press in advance of the event. Thus, your photo could be plastered all over the front page of your local paper as the security guard helps you forcibly out of the store.

For added effect, do go back later in the day and try to get a refund for something you've bought earlier.

Another good wheeze is to start your own campaign group. A friend of mine tried this, and managed to get himself voted off the committee inside two months. Look out for people like this in your circle of friends.

Protesting, like so many aspects of our society, is moving forward into the technological age. The rise of the Internet has brought with it many a useful tool for Seekers on the Path – amongst them is the relatively new phenomenon of "flash mobbing". This is where people use the Internet to publicise a protest event (or a non-event) of some sort, and millions of people turn up at a pre-arranged time to, for example, view a bit of carpet in a particular shop window (this apparently happened at a shop in New York). Imagine the humiliation value if millions of people turned up to watch you shave your legs.

UFO spotting

This one is growing in popularity, so do try to get started in it before it becomes too trendy. There is little humiliation to be gained from involvement in a trendy activity – far better to find one where the humiliation factor is high before you even leave the house. UFOs are known to be attracted to airport regions – probably because they want to study our technology.

Grab a couple of sceptical friends (no humiliation to be had if they actually believe in UFOs), drag them out to the local airport and watch the lights which mysteriously appear in the sky. Make startled exclamations like, "Wow! No earthly craft can manoeuvre like that!"

Try not to be too disheartened when it turns out to be a 747.

Chapter 5
House Renovations

To be absolutely certain of humiliation, it's best to embark on any DIY yourself, and only call in the professionals when it becomes apparent that you are totally out of your depth.

Inspiration
- Failure doesn't have to be permanent – but red wine on the carpet usually does.
- A journey of a thousand workmen starts with a single loose tile.
- Everyone is bad at something. Find your gift.
- The only thing stopping you is common sense.
- When you hit rock bottom, don't think you can sink no further.
- People who live in glass houses… are basically exhibitionists.
- Tomorrow is another day. And the plumber still won't turn up.
- To err is human. To really screw things up you need an architect.

Application
- You can fool some of the people some of the time, but you can't fool the Buildings Inspector.
- Delete "urgent" from your vocabulary – replace it with "it'll take about three months".
- The wallpaper is always printed upside down.

- The bucket of wallpaper paste is always at the bottom of the ladder where you put your foot.
- The only way to stick to your budget is to glue it to your hand.
- Don't quit while you're ahead – keep going until the housing market has crashed.

Buying a property

A cursory glance at the current television schedules will show that the latest craze to grip the country is the art of climbing what is laughingly called the property ladder. In reality it's not a ladder at all, it's a rotten floorboard that you will probably fall through.

The idea is to buy a dump of a house, do it up cheaply, and sell at a vast profit a few months later. Get it right, and soon you could be sipping champagne on the French Riviera, reaping the benefits of all your hard work. Or so the TV programmes would have us believe.

Those of us with a little more imagination, however, will see immediately the possibilities for humiliation. You should start by applying for a mortgage. Here you will have to deal with some spotty youth in the local branch of your bank. You will have to tell him how much you earn, and when he's finished laughing he'll tell you how little they're prepared to lend you.

When dealing with mortgage companies, it is essential to have an understanding of mortgage terminology. They will take your application so much more seriously if you are able to talk confidently about capped rates and interest only trackers. Here are a few definitions to help you:
- Negative equity – not being a member of the actors' union.
- Flexible mortgage – you'll have to bend over backwards to get one.

- Repossession – a property with a ghost.
- Discharge – something to see the doctor about.
- APR – A Proper Rip-off.

Once you start looking for your dream home it is inevitable that you will come into contact with estate agents. It will be helpful to learn their language, too. Here are a few of their favourite phrases:

- Much sought-after location – it's not on the map.
- Full of character – a squatter has moved in.
- In need of some modernisation – like a roof.

When viewing prospective properties it is vital to give the impression that you are an expert in property developing. It will help if you can ask knowledgeable questions such as, "Does it have a DPC?"

When the vendor asks what you mean, you will have to admit that you don't actually know what DPC stands for; you just thought it sounded good.

Other ways to humiliate yourself, or the vendor, while being shown around a prospective purchase:

- Pull off one of their door handles.
- Point out the wallpaper, saying, "I used to have some like that, when it was fashionable."
- Tell them you can't really afford it but your parole officer said it would look better if you settled down and bought a house.
- Say you're looking for a large property with a lot of bedrooms to run your new... erm... business from.

A popular way to buy property nowadays is through an auction, and this is a particularly appealing method for those on the hunt for a real bargain with DIY potential. It's a fairly obvious tactic for anyone in search of humiliation, but if you want a guaranteed result you could try arriving late, bursting into the room waving your mortgage offer, and in a state of haste-induced panic begin bidding immediately on whichever property is on the table.

It is, of course, vitally important not to do any of that boring research stuff. That's for the sad little losers who can't take a joke. We, on the other hand, are seeking the ultimate Enlightenment, and can afford to have a bit of a laugh.

I am reminded of the man who bought a Scottish croft at auction, and only then found out that the fascinating and somewhat archaic laws relating to crofts meant that not only was he forbidden from developing or improving the property, he was also barred from evicting the sitting tenant. We, seekers on the Path, can learn much from this man.

But back to the auction. Here you will notice that the other bidders are employing subtle signals to the auctioneer when making their bids. These might include scratching their nose, winking, or perhaps nodding their heads. Such subtlety is neither required nor desired in seekers on the path to Total Humiliation. You should instead come up with your own unique way to signal the auctioneer. Here are a few simple suggestions:

- Shout "Bingo!"
- Cluck like a chicken.
- Wave your hat in the air.
- Wave your arms in the air.
- Wave your knickers in the air.

You should, of course, be over-enthusiastic in your bidding. Do allow yourself to get carried away in the excitement – there is very little so utterly humiliating as the look on your face when you realise you have bid both more than you can afford, and more than the property is actually worth – and that no-one is bidding against you any more. This, again, is obvious, and you should not need to be told by this stage in your progress.

You should now pull your collar up around your face, make your way hastily to the toilets, and climb out of the window.

Renovations
You will have spent the last few months dealing with estate agents, mortgage advisors, surveyors, and any number of other people who clearly saw it as their duty to prove that you didn't know what you were talking about.

This is where you find out that they were right.

As a general rule, you will under-estimate the cost of renovations 100% of the time. You will usually under-estimate by about 75%, and this will result in a whole raft of people suddenly pointing out that they told you so. This is pretty humiliating when it's just a few of your mates at the local pub, but for complete and utter humiliation, why not approach one of those TV shows that got you hooked on the idea in the first place? They will delight in showing millions of people right across the country what a complete idiot you have been in thinking you could make money on such a venture.

You will, naturally, want to do much of the renovation work yourself, in the completely erroneous belief that it will be cheaper than getting a professional in. In the long run, it is *always* cheaper to get a professional to do the job. But this approach will be humiliating only if you can find a friend who is genuinely good at DIY, and tell him in some detail how it cost you around £5000 to get a professional to fit your new bathroom; when your DIY friend knows he could probably have done it for a little over two hundred quid.

To be absolutely certain of humiliation, it's best to embark on the DIY yourself, and only call in the professionals when it becomes apparent that you are totally out of your depth and have no hope whatsoever of repairing that hole in the wall.

Many DIYers are afflicted with this kind of mental short-circuit, and it is something which has clearly evolved to fulfil an important role in society – that of promoting the economic growth of the small building trade (who are frequently called upon to sort out the mess).

The professional, when he arrives, will snigger at the workmanship and mutter about cowboy builders giving honest traders a bad name. You will, naturally, agree with him wholeheartedly, until he asks for the name of the cowboy builder who screwed up the last job, and you will then be forced to admit that it was in fact you.

The more spectacular the screw-up, the better. Do leave gaping holes in floorboards and three-inch wide gaping channels in the walls where you had once hoped to hide your wiring. Do feel free to knock down walls to reorganise the space inside the property – do not worry too much about whether or not they are load-bearing walls; the answer will become apparent sooner or later.

You will need to invest in a wide range of tools, such as:

- Hot air stripper – entertainment for a bachelor party.
- Electric screwdriver – a type of cocktail.
- Jigsaw – something for those long Sunday afternoons.
- Checked shirt – just because it looks so *cool*.
- Safety goggles – see above.

- Low waist trousers – essential for exposure of well-developed builder's bum.
- Tool belt – for keeping your whisky bottle close at hand.
- Spirit level – a tool for marking how much whisky is left in the bottle.
- Combination square – a complicated type of formation dance.
- Self-grip wrench – the less said the better.

You may be lucky enough to have friends who are willing to lend a hand with the renovations. The only real downside to this is that with more than one person working there, you may lose track of all the jobs.

Always ensure, for example, that the toilet waste pipe has been re-connected before you make use of the facilities. There is much humiliation to be had from removing the bathroom door from its hinges whilst work progresses. No matter how much your friends trust you, they will still feel uncomfortable at using a bathroom where the door has been only temporarily slid back into place so that they can relieve themselves in privacy.

The same sort of thing applies to work carried out on pipes beneath the floorboards. For neatness you will naturally replace the area of floorboards while you work on something else. There is much to be gained from not marking this area with flashing lights or yellow tape. Any innocent person who happens to step on one end of an unsecured floorboard will find themselves unceremoniously dropped about 12 inches to the concrete flooring below.

You would be well advised to invest in a decent security system for your property. Once again, you can save money and increase your level of humiliation by installing it yourself. Begin with locks for the doors and windows. These should be conspicuous and difficult to operate, and you should leave the keys in a "safe" place. This will ensure that you will never see them again.

Now move on to the alarm system. Personally, I would advocate a wireless alarm system since it relies on radio waves which, if handled carefully, can interfere with your television and mobile phone, and will open and close the next-door neighbours' garage door at random.

Once the alarm system has been successfully installed (having paid a professional to come in and sort out the mess you made in attempting it yourself), you will be given a code number to arm and disarm the system. This must not be written down for burglars to find. Unfortunately, this means that you will forget the number, especially when entering the property with guests, or even potential buyers. The sight of you frantically (and uselessly) keying in the cat's date of birth over and over again while alarm bells sound and neighbours gather in the street to see what all the fuss is about, can only enhance your score in the humiliation stakes.

Selling at a profit
You will have spent far more on the renovations than you had originally planned so now you will be trying to increase the market value of your nest egg (or should that be omelette?) by "dressing" it with strategically placed cushions. This will destroy any street cred you may previously have built up. Prospective buyers are guaranteed to open wardrobe doors and cupboards, but will not be expecting a bundle of your knickers to fall on them when they do.

Dressing or staging your property for viewers is all about presentation. Don't forget the more obvious points such as leaving your underwear to air on the clothes dryer; and leaving the remains of last nights' curry in the kitchen, the living room and the bathroom.

If you have a dog or cat, so much the better; especially if they have light-coloured fur. Don't bother to vacuum the chairs, then when prospective buyers sit down they will become covered in cat or dog hairs which will take weeks to remove, and will ensure that your property is one they won't forget in a hurry. You could try to help them remove the hairs from their clothing, and follow them from room to room trying to surreptitiously collect the hairs with a roll of sticky tape – but be warned, such behaviour may result in your arrest.

Chapter 6
Transport

Always assume that the aircraft will wait for you.

Inspiration

- If you don't know where you want to go, it doesn't really matter because the bus timetable will be wrong anyway.
- A journey of a thousand blisters starts with missing the bus.
- Your first step will determine the direction of your journey. Unless you get lost.
- Remember, the car park will be full.
- If the car park is not full, the shops will be closed.
- Roadworks are forever.

Application

- Sharing is important. On the bus, remember to share your thoughts on the government, the economy, the weather, the youth of today, etc., etc., etc.
- Sunday drivers are an inevitable part of life.
- Live life in the bus lane.
- Look for opportunities for variety – take a different route to work – get caught up in a brand new traffic jam.

Public transport

The routes to public humiliation are many and varied – and a great number of them are inextricably linked with the basic business of getting from A to B.

The bus is a good place to start if you are new to being humiliated. The bus driver will do most of the work for you. First, make sure you are carrying something large and awkward, such as a handful of shopping bags, perhaps even a pushchair. Naturally you will not have the correct change, and the driver will not allow you on. Ask if he'll take American Express. Turn to the now impatient queue that will have formed behind you and ask for their help. Engage them in a conversation about what change they may be carrying, and any other random subject that takes your fancy. Very soon, they will decide to take another bus.

When you finally make it onto the bus, you will find it is the wrong bus. If it isn't the wrong bus, you'll probably mis-read the road signs, and get off at the wrong stop.

In the period between boarding the wrong bus and disembarking at the wrong stop you can be secure in the certain knowledge that it is your bus driver's sole purpose in life to aid you in your quest for humiliation. He (or she) will ensure that the bus starts moving before you have found a vacant seat and stashed your shopping or pushchair in the space provided. You will then be sent hurtling to the rear of the bus, bumping into half a dozen other passengers who will be similarly afflicted. Just as you regain your balance and make another tentative move towards an empty seat, he will slam on the brakes and send you hurtling to the front again, whereupon he will glare at you for having the audacity to invade his space, and will deliver a lecture on the health and safety implications for passengers who do not remain seated when the bus is in motion.

Other ways to humiliate yourself on the bus:
- Try getting out your ticket whilst strap-hanging with one hand, and holding three carrier bags with the other.
- Talk to any of the other passengers.
- Take an inquisitive child who will ask you embarrassing questions about the other passengers, and make comments like, "That lady's ugly," or, "That's a fat man."
- Offer the driver a £20 note for your 70p fare.
- Use the time to practise telling jokes to yourself – do make sure you laugh at them.

It is important to inject some variety into your humiliation schedule, and you may like to try your hand at some other modes of public transport. Here is a list of some of the more obvious things you could do to humiliate yourself when travelling by train:
- Expect it to arrive on time.
- Expect to find a seat.
- Eat the food.
- Don't buy a ticket, but then justify this by not using a seat – sit cross-legged on the floor instead and begin your meditation.

Once you have fully humiliated yourself on the ground, you may want to switch to air travel. This will open up many fresh avenues for you.

Always assume that the aircraft will wait for you. All that nonsense about checking in two hours before take off is just petty-minded bureaucracy – the airline staff are annoyed because you're off on holiday, while they have to stay here and deal with lost luggage, screaming kids, and drunken passengers. This is their way of getting revenge (that, and losing your luggage).

Always work on the principle that you may never see your luggage again, so take as much as you can in your hand baggage – magazines, toothbrush, thermos flask… that sort of thing.

Once on board you will find yourself wedged in tightly between two complete strangers. The airline company doesn't really want you leaving your seat and walking up the aisle – it just makes the aircraft look untidy.

If you have taken along a book to read, you will find you are seated next to someone who wants to talk for the entire journey. If, on the other hand, you are prepared for a nice friendly chat, you will find you are sitting next to someone who cannot talk because their entire body, jaw included, is rigid with terror at the prospect of flying. You will have to enlist the stewardess's help in prying his fingers off your arm so that you can visit the bathroom.

Wherever possible your Captain will endeavour to fly above bad weather, but it is inevitable that you will hit the occasional air pocket, which will result in your dinner jumping off the plate and onto your shirt. Do not try to crawl on your knees to retrieve an escaped plastic spoon. The stewardess will be happy to provide you with a new one.

After the meal you may want to recline your seat and take a short nap. This means that the poor passenger sitting behind you will have to finish their meal with a close-up view of your dandruff/bald spot.

People who work on airports are a strange lot, and we can learn much from them. Here are a few examples:

The airline Captain who walked towards his aircraft waving a white stick.

The steward who announced, "We won't be long, we're just trying to sober up the pilot."

The Captain who made his public announcement about cruising speed and altitude, then continued with, "If you look out of the left-hand side window you will see a North Sea Oil Rig..." only to discover he was pressing the wrong button on the transmitter, and his broadcast was not being heard by his passengers at all. Instead, it was being picked up by Air Traffic Control and half a dozen other aircraft, many of whom proceeded to reply that they couldn't see the Oil Rig out of their left window.

An interesting option to bear in mind for the future is space travel. At least one forward-looking holiday company is already considering the possibilities of package holidays to the moon. It will do no harm at all to prepare yourself for the opportunities for humiliation that would be offered by such a venture.

First, do watch Apollo 13 before you go. Remember, your pilot will not be as well trained as Jim Lovell – he will probably be a former package holiday pilot who had to take early retirement following his nervous breakdown caused by all those awkward passengers who turned up late for holiday flights on his 747.

Learning to drive

There are those learner drivers who are so afraid of speed that they drive at 18 mph on a perfectly straight road, and slam the brakes on when someone pulls out a mile in front of them. Others will have no fear at all and will cruise along at 80 mph while the instructor hides under the seat. Whichever category you fall into, learning to drive will present endless opportunities for humiliation.

Do allow a family member to teach you to drive. That way you won't feel at all guilty at arguing with them and abandoning the car on the central reservation.

When the big day of your driving test arrives, do make sure you are running late. All too often in stressful situations your nerves will get the better of you, and the image presented to the world does not even remotely resemble the way you see yourself. There are a few essential steps you should take to overcome this problem and ensure your examiner gets to see the *real* you:

- Play some of your favourite music to relax yourself. Do not worry if the examiner seems not to share your taste in music. Remember, this is *your* day. Turn the volume up and sing along. Don't forget to headbang if this is appropriate to the music.
- Crash the gears.
- Wave at your friends as you speed past them.
- Make sure you have mastered the 49-point turn – the examiner cannot fail to be impressed by the effort you have put in.

Buying a car

Whether you opt for the local garage showroom or the auctions you should always appear to fully understand the mechanics of the car. If you can talk convincingly about manifolds and big ends you can expect to negotiate a better price. When in conversation with a used car salesman you should remember that he will not notice humiliation when it happens – this is something used car salesmen are immune to, and this talent is in fact a pre-requisite for the job. They just keep grinning at you, whatever you say. This is because their brains are only equipped to calculate how much money they can get out of you, and all extraneous information is simply filtered out. You will, therefore, have to put in extra effort to humiliate yourself. You can try this by using a few choice technical terms which will demonstrate your intimate knowledge of car mechanics, and will so impress the salesman that he will instantly offer you a good price.

- Bearings – this is something you often lose when leaving a car park.
- Bleeding (braking system) – a mild imprecation.
- Bores – people you meet on holiday.
- Crankshaft – what you do with your crankshaft is entirely your own business.
- Driveshaft Gaiter – a deadly type of reptile.
- Grab Handle – excess flab which accumulates around the waist.
- Fast-idle adjustment – what you do when the boss leaves the room.
- Lubrication – something to buy at the chemist.
- Mountings – the highest of these is called Everest.
- Tyres – see Grab Handle, above.

Here are some important features to look for when buying a car – these are the points which will ensure your car really stands out from the crowd:

- Electric windows – essential for humiliation, you can spend half an hour opening and closing them before you finally get them to stop half-way down. This works particularly well if you try it when stopped at traffic lights. The average traffic light stays on red for two minutes, while getting the windows to the half-open position takes at least 27 minutes. The queue of angry traffic which builds up behind you in this period can only enhance your humiliation.

- Air conditioning – holes in the floor caused by rust.
- Sun roof – to heat the top of your head and so increase irrational behaviour.
- Radio – ensure yours has an automatic search facility so it can scan the airwaves to facilitate consistent exposure to excruciating music.
- Heater – blows icy cold air in winter, and boils the skin in summer.

Once you have taken the plunge and bought your car, you can look forward to many happy years of blissful motoring. You will learn early on that it is worth knowing if your car runs on petrol or diesel. It can be a little embarrassing to explain such a mistake to the RAC man. Likewise, he will find it immensely amusing if it turns out the reason your car won't start is because you have run out of fuel.

As your vehicle ages, so the likelihood of it breaking down at some point increases. When that fateful day arrives, you will be on your way somewhere important, and therefore will be dressed inappropriately for the weather. You will, for example, be wearing a smart, dry-clean only, outfit, and will not be equipped with Wellingtons for the two inches of rain water you will have to wade through to reach a telephone (your mobile will have a flat battery, naturally).

In winter your locks will freeze up. This is fine if you are at home and have ready access to a supply of hot water. If you have been out for the evening, however, you may find yourself struggling. Do not follow the example of the man who decided to pee on the lock to defrost it. Bare skin and frozen metal do not go well together and although Total Humiliation was achieved in this instance, it was not without a great deal of pain. If your locks do freeze up, you will be glad if you chose a hatchback, as it is possible to climb in through the boot. All you lose is your dignity.

Back-seat driving

Back-seat driving is more art than science. In expert hands, this is a powerful technique for humiliating your friends. In addition to giving your friend unnecessary directions and alerting their attention to the presence of buses on the road, you should also endeavour to whimper. This shows what confidence you have in their driving abilities. Do cling to the roof handle with one hand, and the handbrake with the other.

Chapter 7
Modern Technology

*The more contact you have with computers,
the more chance you have of being totally humiliated.*

Inspiration
- Your computer is only as good as the idiot who programmed it.
- A persistent error message is technology's way of inducing a coronary.
- Life is hard... then you get a computer.
- All good things come to an end – let us pray this also applies to the Internet.
- The off button is there for a reason.
- The software will be obsolete by the time you have finished loading it.
- If it doesn't work, it's *your* fault.
- Remember, failure is not an option – it's a design feature.

Application
- If it ain't broke – take a sledgehammer to it.
- Computer problems will disappear the minute the engineer comes to look at it, and will mysteriously re-appear two minutes after he has left. This also applies to televisions.

- If it should ever become necessary for you to remain motionless for hours at a time, try ringing up a call centre.
- Nothing in life is certain, except death, taxes, and computer crashes.
- If it's impossible for it to go wrong, your computer will find a way.
- The office photocopier knows when you are using it for personal stuff. This is when it is most likely to break down. This is also when the boss is most likely to wander over and take an interest in your work.

Modern technology

Modern technology is specifically designed to make you look ridiculous, and the more of it you have, the more easily this can be achieved.

- Do you have boxes full of betamax videos lurking at the back of your garage?
- Do 8-track cassettes still collect dust in your loft?
- Do you think the Internet is just a phase?
- When Sony first brought out the Playstation, did you say it would never catch on?
- Do you think electric car windows have a mind of their own?
- Do your bathroom scales lie to you?
- Do you ever wonder if maybe the Luddites had a point?
- Do you feel the need to swear at your computer more than once a day?

If so, you clearly have a genetic predisposition towards making an idiot of yourself, and are already utilising modern technology to facilitate this important end result. Your progress on the Path is assured.

Computer games systems, you will have noticed, have a life of about two months before they're superseded by something more expensive. You've barely got the thing out of the box and plugged in before it's obsolete, and suddenly it's impossible to buy games or spare parts. Is this a cunning tactic on the part of benevolent computer games manufacturers to help us on our way towards Enlightenment?

The humiliation starts when you enter the shop to buy your new games system. Here you will be faced with a spotty youth who will treat you with utter contempt simply for having the audacity to be middle-aged (in the eyes of your average computer games sales person, this means anybody older than about 20). This is born of a deep-seated resentment because you can buy beer in the local off-licence and he can't. Clearly, at such an advanced age, you cannot be expected to function in society, and the pre-pubescent shop assistants will have been trained to deal with people such as yourself. The training gives them two choices; they can either patronise you, or they can baffle you. Whichever option they choose will ultimately result in your humiliation, and this can be further enhanced if you try to demonstrate your knowledge of computer games systems by referring fondly to the old tennis game that went blip...blip...blip...blipblip.

Having survived the humiliation of being sold the games system that the spotty youth wanted to sell you (rather than the one you *thought* you wanted to buy), you will now have the unparalleled pleasure of taking it home and setting it up. It will help enormously if you have an eight-year-old in the house, and if his friends can be present to witness your humiliation as he shows you the right way to install the system, so much the better.

Next, your eight-year-old will proceed to beat you at each and every game you play. You will be forced to resort to quiz games which ask questions about the moon landings, The Beatles and Starsky and Hutch. Now, if you play to win, and do a little victory dance at every question you answer correctly, you will truly be on the route to making a fool of yourself.

In fact, even if you quite like modern technology, it is still possible to humiliate yourself with it. There are mobile phones that allow you to send pictures, for example. It doesn't take a particularly fertile imagination to see the possibilities here – it is virtually guaranteed that sooner or later you will send a revealing picture, originally intended only for the eyes of your beloved, to your boss. This is just as humiliating if the recipient is your mother-in-law.

Then there are video recorders. When these were first introduced they were fairly basic, but nevertheless the skill to operate them was bestowed only on a select few, and it helped enormously if you were under the age of 15.

The ability to programme a video recorder is a fragile skill which you will inevitably lose as you get older. This decline continues until you reach Bumbling Idiot status at around the age of 30.

Now video recorders are being replaced with DVDs. It is, frankly, so easy to humiliate yourself when trying to operate one of these, that it's something we hardly need bother with.

Science and scientists

Many people seem to have the impression that scientists are staid, serious people. Nothing could be further from the truth. Scientists are not immune to the effects of humiliation. Indeed, some of them seem to actively court it.

We are all familiar with the Doppler Effect, for example. But less is known about the humiliation Doppler endured, and inflicted on others, in working out his theory. It involved a group of trumpeters, playing on top of a freight train as it moved up and down a track. Anyone attempting such a feat nowadays would expect to find Jeremy Beadle lurking nearby, but that was a more innocent time.

Other famous people have used science to humiliate themselves throughout history. Ben Franklin, for example, chose to fly a kite in a thunderstorm. While we can now appreciate the value of his efforts, he must have looked a bit of a prat at the time. Archimedes is famous for having run down the street naked, and this started quite a trend in the seventies, although most of the participants ended up getting arrested and not contributing much at all to the body of scientific knowledge.

Computers

The more contact you have with computers, the more chance you have of being totally humiliated. You will either lose every important piece of information you need to keep your daily life running smoothly, or you will know it's there somewhere but simply be unable to access it. Or you might inadvertently email it to your boss, who will suddenly realise what you've been doing all that time you said you were working on finance reports.

With these few simple rules in mind, we can greet with open arms the aspirations of a certain large computer company to introduce a system that lets you save every photo, every letter, every telephone conversation, indeed every memory, into a database. What happens when that system becomes obsolete? Or when someone hacks into it?

Pick up a few little snippets of such information and you can quite easily develop your own conspiracy theory. It is now an accepted fact that developing, and talking about, a conspiracy theory *always* leads to you being either humiliated or certified. This is, therefore, a recommended hobby for Seekers on the Path.

Some people, of course, have long been aware of the sinister implications of becoming too dependent on computers. These people are no less prone to humiliation, however. There are many well-documented instances of such individuals being pushed to their very limits and finally succumbing to the anti-technology feelings which reside deep in the uncharted recesses of the human soul; and actually shooting their computer (or sometimes the bank's computer, which obviously results in rather more paperwork).

To humiliate yourself, without necessarily ending up in jail, you might try simply yelling at your computer. If you do this in a crowded office, or indeed in your bank, you cannot fail to be totally and completely humiliated – though this will probably not become apparent until you have stopped yelling and realised that everyone is watching you in stony silence.

You can further humiliate yourself by using computer jargon which you do not fully understand. To help you along, here are a few simple definitions:

- CD ROM – seedy room (probably your office).
- Ram – uncastrated male sheep. It remains unclear what this has to do with computers, but the term is in common use, so it must be worth dropping into conversations.
- Booting – kicking the computer when it doesn't work.
- Re-booting – kicking it again.

- Hard drive – any journey when your car radio is broken, and there are no service stations where you might get a nice cup of tea.
- Backup – if your computer crashes, losing all your work, this is bound to get your back up.
- Browser – someone who is not a serious purchaser.
- Field properties – barn conversions, that sort of thing.
- Buggered – a technical term describing the status when your computer is no longer facilitating synergistic functionalities or delivering mission-critical technologies.
- Click and drag – a cabaret act.
- A drive – a pleasant way to spend Sunday afternoon.
- Floppy – a medical problem.
- Desktop – the bit you clear when the cleaner comes to work.

The Internet

This is another example of society moving towards a more widespread basis for humiliation. The growth of the Internet is proof, if proof were needed, that deep down inside, people really *want* to be humiliated. Here are some incredibly easy ways to humiliate yourself in this sphere:

- Believe everything you read on the Internet.
- Invest in a web cam – then people around the world can watch you being inept at any time of the day or night.
- Do your shopping on the Internet. Supermarket shopping on the Internet takes longer than actually going to your local store. It can also prove to be a completely pointless exercise since you can spend two hours filling your online shopping basket with biscuits and cakes to bump your spending up to the minimum required for

free delivery, only to find at the end that the free delivery offer actually applied to electrical goods, and it finished last week anyway. By this time you will have worked yourself up into a nice state of apoplexy, and this can be relieved by ringing up the store's helpline and yelling at some poor bloke who won't have a clue what you're talking about – but he'll put the call on speakerphone so all his colleagues can listen in.

Mobile phones

Don't trust 'em. A government-funded system for tracking your movements every minute of the day. If you tell people about this theory loudly and at length you will soon be well advanced along the Path to Total Humiliation. The theory may, of course, be true, but none of your friends will believe it so you'll end up looking an idiot anyway.

Mobile phone technology is set to provide us with even more ways to humiliate ourselves. In Japan they're developing a new phone that you wear on your wrist like a watch. It transmits vibrations into the bones in your hand, and this is converted into sound when you stick your finger in your ear.

And all this proves that you're not on your own in your quest for humiliation. High-tech companies are spending vast fortunes on research and development of new and ever more interesting ways to help you look silly.

Bathroom scales

If you are a dignified and respectable person you will keep your bathroom scales locked away under the stairs, behind that exercise bike Auntie Maureen gave you fifteen years ago, if you must have them at all.

We, however, are not interested in dignity – this is incompatible with progress on the path to Total Humiliation. For maximum impact you should invest in a speak-your-weight machine, and set the volume to high when you have guests.

Mirrors
These have a tendency to leap out at you in shops to remind you how dreadful you look. It's hard to maintain any semblance of self-esteem when everywhere you look there's an overweight slob in poorly-fitting clothes whom you suddenly realise is, in fact, you.

Mirrors should be avoided at home – this means you will turn up for work each day without the faintest clue what you look like. Do, however, stand in front of shop mirrors – there is little in life as thoroughly undignified as preening yourself in public.

Reality TV programmes
If you have no talent whatsoever and want to be humiliated in front of a wide audience, this would be an excellent option.

Call centres
Ring up, on a premium rate number, wait in a queue for twenty minutes, finally get through, and then ask why they have overcharged you by 12 pence.

Chapter 8
Other People

*We have already looked at how your children can humiliate you.
Now it's time to turn the tables and learn how
you can humiliate them.*

Inspiration
- You don't have to like people to humiliate them.
- Be yourself. There is no greater humiliating factor.
- A friend in need is a pain in the neck.
- Great minds think alike... and fools seldom differ.
- He who laughs last... is a bit slow on the uptake.

Application
- Become a good listener – then when you know all their secrets you can truly humiliate your friends.
- It has been said you can judge a man by his friends – make sure your friends are idiots.
- Try to vary your routine – do new things with or to your friends – just make sure you don't get arrested.
- Be the weakest link.
- Do unto others before they get the chance to do unto you.

In previous chapters we have looked at ways to humiliate yourself and any friends, strangers or vague acquaintances who may happen to pass your way. We have looked mainly at how this humiliation can be achieved by what you do, and what activities you choose to engage in. It is important, however, not to overlook the potential for humiliation that comes from who you are – and who your friends are.

Let us consider how we can increase our own prospects for humiliation simply by choosing our friends with care.

Elderly relatives
Time spent with your elderly relatives is rarely wasted. They will humiliate you first by insisting that you go to HMV and ask for a Des O'Connor record (elderly relatives make a point of not understanding CD players – so this is humiliating on a number of different levels), and then they will proceed to tell any passing shop assistant how much you weighed when you were born, how many attempts it took you to pass your driving test, and how infrequently you visit. Mothers are particularly good at this.

Remember, your mother has spent your entire life humiliating you (with the best of intentions) and she's not about to stop now that you've left home. If you arrange to meet her for lunch (this being the most efficient way she can ensure you're eating properly), you will pull into the car park to find her standing there, waving as she guards an empty parking space for you. She will then guide you inch-by-inch into the space.

Later, she will ring you at work and launch into conversation without checking that it's actually you who has picked up the phone.

She will be fiercely protective of her grandchildren, and will accompany you to school events so that she can say things like, "Isn't that the little tart who punched my grandson?" while pointing to a seven-year-old with pigtails.

Now that you have moved out and she has more free time she will take on a sudden new lease of life, and join a gym. She'll be fitter than you and better dressed than you, and she'll most certainly have a better social life than you. Try going for a jog and wallow in the humiliation to be found in being out-run by an eighty-year-old.

Young relatives

They have to be relatives, because very few young people will be prepared to waste their time on the likes of you, unless they're related by blood and so feel some sort of obligation.

No-one likes to admit that they are getting old, so if you have young relatives you will naturally align yourself with them. They will take you to concerts where you will complain that the music is too loud. This statement will have a curiously familiar ring to it, echoing as it does, something lost in the distant memory of your youth – but you will not see the significance until you find yourself also commenting that the policemen are looking younger these days.

Eager to fit in with your young friends, you will accompany them to the gym, where just climbing the stairs to the reception desk will leave you gasping for breath.

You will throw away your tattered old jeans because they have a hole in the knee, only to find your young friend has just spent a fortune on the latest fashion – jeans with a hole in the knee. Young people will happily spend on a shirt what you spend on your mortgage.

And finally, you will find yourself lamenting the drought of '76, whereupon they will gaze at you in bewilderment and say, "I wasn't born then".

Wild friends
These are the ones who like to flash their boobs at complete strangers in the pub, and will do pretty much anything for a free drink. The mere fact that you know them will enhance your score on the humiliation-o-meter.

If you get one of these wild friends drunk enough, she'll do the "tiger feet" dance with you. A whole group of you doing it would be okay, but just the two of you is excruciatingly humiliating, and any witnesses will never let you live it down.

Posh friends
They don't have children. They don't have housework. They just have neat, ordered lives, and beige carpet. You will never find any dust or coffee rings in their homes; and you will live in dread of them turning up unannounced on your doorstep, because of course, you *do* have dust in your house. Spend more than twenty minutes in their company and you will feel totally humiliated. It wears off, though, so you'll have to keep going back to be further humbled.

Posh friends will expect you to remove your shoes whenever you enter their immaculate homes. Do make sure you have chosen to wear a pair of socks with a large hole for your big toe to stick through. This will be greatly appreciated by your friends, who will try to hold a pleasant conversation with you, but despite their best efforts they will be unable to keep their eyes off your protruding big toe.

At social get-togethers there is always some poor sod who manages to spill their drink on the sofa. Let it be you.

Random friends
It is worth cultivating friendships with a wide variety of people, so you can invite them to important events, and then bask in the humiliation of simply knowing them. In the pursuit of the widest possible range of acquaintances it may be necessary to move in social circles not normally available to you. Mixing with such diverse groups as say, martial artists, and watercolour artists, can only enrich your life. The experience will leave you a more rounded, multi-faceted, character, equipped to humiliate yourself and your friends in many different spheres. Here are some examples:

- The Trekkie – in fact this applies to virtually any sci-fi buff. They appear perfectly normal, ordinary people, until the question of Mr Spock's parentage is raised. At this point they will gleefully admit to having every single episode on tape, and will bore you rigid with a million little-known facts. One sure route to self-humiliation is to confess to being a fan yourself. They will *always* know more than you.
- The Protester – always carries a multi-purpose banner and ready-made speech. The experienced protesters are okay, it's the newly converted ones that you have to avoid. These are, perversely, the easiest to humiliate, however. You can try the verbal equivalent of painting them into a corner by picking careful holes in their belief-system. If your chosen protester is an anti-vivisectionist, for example, and refuses to use products tested on animals – why are they smoking?

- The Pro-hunt Lobbyist – an experienced self-humiliator. Question their activities and they will launch into a defence about efficiently curbing the fox population, yet when you mention cruelty they come up with, "Don't worry, we hardly ever catch anything." It takes a rare gift to be able to utter both sentences in the same breath.
- The New Mum – will tell everyone in great detail how she came to conceive, and then go on to describe the birth (giving a demonstration of the use of stirrups). Naturally, she will be carrying an extensive supply of photos with which to bore everyone she meets. New mums fall in two categories. First, the chaotic, frazzled, desperate type who remind you of yourself. Second, the type who have their daily routine organised on a minute-by-minute basis, and will happily tell you how you've been doing it wrong all these years. She will go on to tell you that her new baby sleeps right through the night (your own children will have been in full time education before they managed this feat).
- The Intellectual – will talk incomprehensively about dark matter, particle accelerators and nanotechnology.
- The Delinquent – will drink too much and pick a fight with absolutely *everybody*.
- The Cryptozoologist – will be able to deliver a lecture (whether asked to or not) on the likelihood of the Loch Ness Monster actually being a plesiosaur, the Yeti and Bigfoot being related species, and the total length of the last Giant Squid to have been found. This is okay if the other people present are interested in the subject, but that would be rather pointless, wouldn't it? Instead, invite your cryptozoologist friend along to a meeting with your bank manager. The loan application is bound to be looked upon

favourably when you demonstrate your excellent judgement in choosing friends.

Children

We have already looked at how your children can humiliate you. Now it's time to turn the tables and learn how *you* can humiliate *them*. Here are a few simple suggestions.

- Be the only mother who waits outside school to wave them off on their weekly trip to the swimming baths.
- Dance at the school disco.
- Sing.
- Kiss them goodbye in the playground each morning.
- Use baby-talk and pet names like Mummy's Special Hero.
- Make your child carry a walkie-talkie, and insist that they call in to give their location every five minutes.
- Chat to their friends.
- Cook for their friends.

Animals

There are many different ways that your animals might contribute to your general level of humiliation, such as savaging your visitors' coats, leaving little presents on your neighbours' doorstep, or developing an unnatural interest in the postman's left leg.

Cats, being a wonderfully bloody-minded species, will do exactly what they want, exactly when they want, and this can lead to all kinds of fun.

I am reminded of the man who once, for reasons best known to himself, tried to incite his dog to chase my cat. "Look, Fido," he said,

"Catsssssss!" and pointed to my moggie, who was minding his own business, watching the birds in the trees. Once the hissing and snarling alerted the moggie to what was going on, he naturally did what any self-respecting cat would do. He arched his back, hissed, and chased the dog down the road. The dog owner was, no doubt, extremely grateful for this incident, which left him mortally humiliated, and with a healthy respect for felines.

Let's look at another situation. What is the correct action to take when your cat and next door's ginger tom are recreating a scene from Tom and Jerry (the one where all you can see is a whirling circle and a cloud of dust – and the surrounding air is punctuated with tufts of flying fur)? Do you:

- Panic
- Run away
- Go back inside and check what action the cat care books recommend
- Scream like a fishwife and chase them down the street

Your response to this question will give an indication of how far you have progressed along the Path. It is in everyday events such as this that we can begin to form the habit of humiliation, so do not overlook the opportunities which are presented to you day to day.

Do defend your cat's good reputation, and vehemently deny that he has anything whatsoever to do with the diminishing contents of your next door neighbour's fish pond. Your cat will come wandering home, probably even as you are in the midst of your defence speech, with both front legs soaking wet, and a goldfish in his mouth. Cats have an uncanny knack for this sort of timing, and will also endeavour to drag a starling through the garden just as you are telling your neighbours that he is getting old and is no threat whatsoever to the local wildlife.

Dogs tend to be slightly more amenable to doing what you ask of them, so perhaps it's even more humiliating if you have a dog that won't. My dog, for example, used to love attending dog obedience classes. She didn't actually take part in them – she just liked to sit on my knee and watch. I'd take her out for walks but we never got further than the end of the street before she got scared and turned for home.

This was okay on dark winter evenings, but was somewhat embarrassing in the bright sunshine of a pleasant summer day, with all the neighbours peeping out through their net curtains.

For enhanced opportunities for humiliation it is recommended that you enrol your pooch in a dog agility class. This way you can both demonstrate your ineptitude in front of an admiring crowd of onlookers, and perhaps even the local press.

Most dogs love agility courses, with jumps and tunnels set up for them to negotiate. It's great fun. The only problem is that your dog won't understand that he's supposed to go round the obstacles in a specific pre-determined order.

This kind of free-thinking approach to competition is also disapproved of in equine circles. If your inclination is towards horse-riding, do enter yourself in the local gymkhana where you can publicly display your prowess at falling off.

You may, of course, prefer more exotic pets. Large spiders or snakes should be allowed to roam free in your home. This won't especially humiliate you, but it will have an impressive effect on any guests or door-to-door salesmen.

Chapter 9
Inner Humiliation

Remember, true humiliation comes from within.

Inspiration
- Enjoy today – tomorrow things will only get worse.
- A bird in the hand... will poop on you.
- If you are not sure what direction to take in life... welcome to the club.
- Humiliation doesn't *have* to be in public.
- Humiliation is your friend.
- If you expect nothing, you'll still be disappointed.
- Life is just a bowl.

Application
- Don't be yourself. Be someone else.
- Grin a lot. It makes people suspicious.
- Set yourself realistic goals like "Today I will bring about world peace". Reward yourself with a bar of chocolate when you achieve these goals.
- Add "Oops," to your vocabulary.
- If you are having trouble getting started on a task, make a list of all the reasons why you should do it, and then all the reasons why

you shouldn't. By the time you have finished the list it will be too late to do the task anyway. Problem solved.
- It is perfectly acceptable to say "Well done" to yourself – but slightly unsettling if you reply.

Self-esteem

The mysteries of self-esteem are usually the preserve of the self-appointed lifestyle gurus. If you have been following the instructions in this book carefully you will need no guidance here. Your self-esteem will be minimal. Enlightenment is within your grasp.

In simple terms, self-esteem is just the phrase we use to describe what we think of ourselves, and how we fit into the social hierarchy. Self-help books will provide you with many ideas and pointers for improving the way you perceive yourself. Face facts – these techniques do not apply to you. If, to choose a fairly typical exercise as an example, you stand in front of the mirror for ten minutes each day saying, "I *can* do it. I *am* successful," someone is bound to come in and catch you sooner or later. This technique is therefore highly recommended for Seekers on the Path, although you might want to change the mantra to something like, "Why me?" or "It's all going wrong again."

This section looks at how we can lower self-esteem by the way we dress, and the way we behave. Remember, true humiliation comes from within. You don't actually need to be in the presence of others to be humiliated. For those with skill and dedication, who have studied the art of humiliation long and hard, it is a way of life; an intrinsic quality to be treasured.

Personality disorders

It is immensely helpful if you can develop one or two minor neuroses. This way neighbours will regularly see you checking you have locked the front door, and then popping back just to make *really* sure you've locked it. If you are truly accomplished in this area you can use the same technique on the car, but be warned it can be expensive when the handle comes off in your hand. This sort of thing is of benefit on two levels. Firstly it makes you look an idiot to any independent observer. And secondly it makes you late for *everything*.

Try to develop a daily routine. It will quickly become habit, and you will find you can make a complete fool of yourself without even thinking about it. Here is a step-by-step guide to get you started:

- Before leaving the house check all the windows are closed.
- Check again.
- Check you haven't left any taps running.
- Check you have turned off the cooker and the fire and the kettle and the lights.
- Check again.
- Take a deep breath.
- Exit.
- Lock the door.
- Pull on the door handle, counting three pulls. Do this three times.
- Walk away from the door.
- Go back to check you have *really* turned off the cooker.
- Exit again and repeat the process with the door handle. If you are distracted it is vitally important that you start all over again.
- Finally, walk to the car.
- Stop. Realise you have left your car keys in the house. Swear.

- Go back to get them.
- Before leaving the house check all the windows are closed.

And so on.

Personal appearance
While true humiliation comes from within, it doesn't hurt to screw up your appearance as well. Packaging, as they say, is everything.

Hair salons are essential tools for humiliation. The subjugation of the ego begins the moment you walk through the door and are confronted by a group of people who quite clearly see it as their duty to look down on you. Their own hair may very well look like a bird's nest in the aftermath of a tornado, but they will still manage to find fault with yours. They will dress you in the least flattering floral tent they can find, and proceed to point out split ends and dandruff, and comment on the poor-quality cut you had last time (somewhere else, of course).

Here are some tips for enhanced humiliation. These will work particularly well if you can do them shortly before you visit the hair salon:
- Cut your own hair. You will inevitably make a mess of it. Remember, uneven cuts are only acceptable if they have been done by a professional, in which case it's innovative and exciting. If you do it yourself it's just *bad*. If you have very short hair you might like to shave in a design of some kind to express your individuality. This, again, is a field where professional screw-ups are okay, but do-it-yourself jobs will render you terminally uncool.
- Colour your own hair. See above. It's only okay to have pink hair if you have paid a lot of money for it.

- Perm your own hair. This one is particularly recommended. You will quickly learn that you cannot reach the back of your head, so it's advisable to rope in a friend. This way, you can put the curlers in one side of your head, and your friend can do the other. Only when you have finished will you discover that you have been winding the hair round the curlers more tightly than your friend so you will have loose, flowing angel curls on one side, and an afro on the other.

Clothes

Do not worry about fashion. If you hold on to something long enough it will always come back into fashion eventually. This is the point at which you should donate it to charity and start wearing something else.

Indecision is another skill which you could usefully develop. It is recommended that you buy clothes on impulse, since first instincts are often the best. Then take your purchases home and consider at leisure if they really deserve to become a permanent part of your wardrobe. Remember, as long as you leave the tags on, there remains the possibility that you can return them. This is called "keeping your options open". The flipside of this is that by the time you have decided that you really do like that suede jacket, it will be out of style. This is called "stupid".

An added benefit to delaying your final decision about a purchase is that it is inevitable that one day you will leave home in a hurry and dash to the office to give a presentation – only later will you discover that the price tag has been hanging down the back of the jacket the entire time.

They say that you can tell a lot about a person by what they wear. Your clothing is simply the outward expression of your personality. Remember what fun dressing up was when you were a child? This was before the social conditioning had completely stripped away any sense of individuality and you started worrying about what was "cool".

Fashion designers have been helping people to look stupid for centuries. If you have any doubts, take a look at the following list:

- The bustle – a device to make women's bums look bigger.
- The codpiece – a device to draw attention to a man's inadequacy.
- Shoulder pads – to enhance the similarities to a Fokker Friendship aircraft.
- Platform Shoes – something to fall over in.
- The Puffball Skirt – a brief triumph of design over common sense.
- Stiletto heels – for sinking into the tarmac on a hot summer day.

Dieting

Do announce it to the world when you decide to embark on a diet. It is important that as many people as possible know about it when you fail. I say *when* and not *if*, because, after all, there is little humiliation to be gained in starting on a diet and sticking to it. No one wants to hear about people who are self-disciplined and controlled and who manage to lose two pounds a week, and now have a wonderful new lifestyle as a result. You will not achieve enlightenment by sticking to a diet.

Diets are not meant to be fun. They are designed to humiliate, especially if you join one of those clubs where they weigh you in front of the whole class each week and announce how much weight you have gained. Perhaps you could go one step further, and get on to a television diet show so the entire nation can be witness to your appalling lack of willpower.

Remember, if your mind is consumed by thoughts of food, you will have no time or energy to consider enlightenment. Eat a reasonable sort of diet with the odd chocolate cake thrown in here and there, and then your mind will be free to consider higher matters.

Inner humiliation

True humiliation, as has already been said, comes from within. Do not be influenced by those feckless types who may make a great show of being humiliated when it suits them, only to shake off the heavy, rough-hewn, cloak of self-humiliation in favour of the more silken wrap of confidence and success the first time humiliation looks like it might get in the way of their social life. For genuine Seekers on the Path, humiliation is not something we can escape so lightly, and nor should we try.

Firstly, you should try to always believe that you *can* do it, whatever it is. Tell all your friends that you fully intend climbing Everest on a pogo stick, or becoming a rock star. This way, when you fail, everyone will notice, and this is far more humiliating than if you had kept your big mouth shut.

Remember, the world is full of people who have never done anything remarkable, and who have never told their friends that they intended to do anything remarkable. There is no humiliation in such an approach. Here are some general hints and tips to help you find the Path:

- Play monopoly/football with your young nephew... and play to win.
- Revive the Kevin Keegan look.
- Go jogging.
- Talk loudly about your sexual preferences.
- Talk loudly about your friends' sexual preferences.
- Be indecisive.
- Be wrong.

It can be terribly helpful to be socially inept. For example, you may try to compliment a friend by commenting on their new hairstyle. It will inevitably come out wrong. In your mind, you will form the phrase, "That new hairstyle looks great!" but the words you will hear coming out of your mouth will be, "Your hair looks great! Have you washed it?"

Similarly, if your partner asks, "Does my bum look big in this?" you might hear warning bells which lead you to pause and think carefully before you answer. Ignore the bells. The longer you pause, the harder it is to sound convincing when you answer in the negative. Remember, there is only one correct answer to this question, and it has nothing to do with what your eyes are telling you.

AND FINALLY...

There are a number of basic principles you should observe if humiliation is your chosen path to ultimate Enlightenment.

Procrastination is more than just a long word that you can't spell. It is a valuable tool for spreading disorder, for it affects not just your own life, but your friends' as well. It is a useful ploy to combine it with general disorganisation. Using these twin powers wisely will mean that your life is chaotic, your home is untidy, and your office will contain a pile of papers which resembles a small mountain range.

You will, naturally, be short of money, for such is the power of disorder that it will seep into your handling of your budget as well. Such mis-handling will result in letters with nice red ink, and the electricity supply being unexpectedly terminated. As you lie in the dark, amongst a lifetime of clutter, you cannot help but ponder the eternal mysteries of life and how you came to be in this situation.

Your journey has begun.

If you have followed the advice and suggestions in this book carefully, you should by now be fully conversant with the general principles of humiliation. You will have seen that, far from being a subject for dread, humiliation is actually something we all need, a powerful force which we can all tap into if we focus our energy. I trust that I leave you well equipped to proceed on your own to ever greater heights of humiliation.